The Business
of Re-Roofing

The Business of Re-Roofing

◆

An Owner's Manual

Neal Middleton

iUniverse, Inc.
New York Lincoln Shanghai

The Business of Re-Roofing
An Owner's Manual

Copyright © 2007 by Neal Middleton

iUniverse books may be ordered through booksellers or by contacting:

iUniverse
2021 Pine Lake Road, Suite 100
Lincoln, NE 68512
www.iuniverse.com
1-800-Authors (1-800-288-4677)

Before following any suggestions contained in this book, you should consult your professional builder and financial advisor. Neither the author nor the publisher shall be liable or responsible for any loss or damage allegedly arising as a consequence of your use or application of any information or suggestions in this book.

ISBN: 978-0-595-43387-2 (pbk)
ISBN: 978-0-595-87713-3 (ebk)

Printed in the United States of America

To Deryl, my wife, my partner in life for over 31 years. You let me dream, and when my dreams didn't come true, you didn't judge me harshly. You hugged me and told me that you loved me. You stuck by me, through the drinking, through the repossessed houses, through the repossessed cars, and through the unfulfilled promises.

I love you more than life. I need you more than air. You are my best friend. You are my life. May you never lay down your head at night doubting that you are loved.

Neal

And to my kids, Jonathan and Carrie, who didn't disown me when they unwrapped their Christmas packages to find only an IOU inside. You were both better children than I deserved. And today, you are both better parents than I ever was. There is no way that I can put into words how proud I am of you, or how much I love you.

Dad

Contents

Foreword!

Marty Haight

Marty Haight is the owner and CEO of one of the most successful residential roofing companies in the country. His companies will do over 100 million in residential re-roofing gross sales in 2006.

I have invested in a lot of business ventures. I've made money on some and lost money on others. That is the nature of business. The one I remember as the best investment I've ever made (other than my own companies) was in a little start-up roofing company in Wisconsin. The principal partner and chief operating officer was Neal Middleton. I received a great return on that investment, even though I didn't contribute much to the effort. That wasn't a surprise. I knew Neal. He had worked for me for several years.

Neal has this thing down to a science. If you own or manage a local roofing company, I would listen to him if I were you.

Marty Haight

◆   ◆   ◆

John Francis
Owner of Northern Virginia Roofing

In May of 2003, re-roofing was a small part of my business. The main focus of my roofing company was repairs. That changed when a friend of mine introduced me to Neal and Deryl Middleton. I met them, I hired them, I fell in love with them, and the rest is history. Neal's business philosophy began to kick in quickly. My repair sales increased, and my re-roofing business began growing almost exponentially. We finished 2003 at 2.1 million in re-roofing gross sales. That grew to 4.5 million in 2004, and to almost 8 million in 2005. We're on pace to do over 10 million in 2006. I'm not sure where it will end, but I can't wait to find out.

Neal and Deryl are very special people. Listen to them. Learn from them. And then sit back and enjoy the ride. Thank you Neal and Deryl. We miss you more than we can put into words.

John Francis

◆   ◆   ◆

Seth Peyser

Seth Peyser is the owner of Stroudsburg Door and Trim, StairCo, and Stroudsburg Roofing, all located in Stroudsburg, Pennsylvania, in the Pocono Mountains near the New Jersey border.

I met Neal at a roofing exposition in Florida. He was trying to sell me his roofing estimate software, but I needed more than that. I needed someone to teach me how to run my roofing business and make it profitable. I convinced Neal to come to Pennsylvania to help me out. He was only there five months, but I can't describe to you the difference he made in my company in that short time. He tore it down to nothing, and then he rebuilt it. Now, my roofing company is running smoothly, and it is very profitable. I will never be able to thank him enough.

Seth Peyser

Acknowledgements

Marty for showing me that making money in business and being a good and decent person are not mutually exclusive endeavors.

John and Kimberly for being courageous enough to let me experiment with your company and your money. You care about your people. That alone justifies your being set atop any list of those worth emulating. The world without you in it would be less worth living in.

Seth for challenging me and making me reach deep and commit before rubber-stamping my intended course of action. You made me a better manager in the process. And for forcing yourself to keep listening while I finished a point, even though you had already understood and processed it before I had it half articulated.

Kay and Nicky, for being two of the very special people God used to bless the earth, and for hanging in there when you thought I was just a loser that John had hired to make your life miserable.

Kathy, aka "Roofer Chick", for saying the words that I'm sure you won't even remember. After watching me give a presentation in the field, you said, "Neal, I would buy a roof from you."

To my guys, especially **Jeremiah**, **Rob**, **Ryan**, **Joe, and Kevin**. Thank you for making me look so smart.

To the wives of my guys, especially **Jocelyn, Danielle, Thao, and Stephanie**. You are as much a part of what they've accomplished as they are, or I am.

And finally, to all of those listed here, thank you for being such wonderful friends to both Deryl and me. Knowing you has enriched our lives beyond measure.

Introduction

Why write a book telling people who already own and operate a roofing company how to own and operate a roofing company? Obviously, they know or they wouldn't be in business, right?

I'm not interested in helping the guy who's making a million a year, make three. I'm interested in helping the guy who's working his ass off and still losing money, turn a profit.

I'm interested in helping the guy who's working his ass off to break even, earn a nice profit.

I'm interested in helping the guy who's working his ass off to make two hundred grand, make five or six or seven or more.

To hell with the guy who's already making over a million a year. He needs to go fishing.

◆　　◆　　◆

A shingle manufacture's rep told me about one of his customers, the owner of a roofing company in southern Virginia. "Neal, he really needs help. Would you stop in and talk to him?" I did, and after closing the door to his office, the owner of the company sat down, put his elbows on his desk, looked me right in the eyes and said, "We did over seven million in sales last year and I didn't make any money." I almost fell out of my chair.

◆　　◆　　◆

I set up a booth at the 2004 International Roofing Exposition in Orlando, Florida to peddle my estimate software. Seth Peyser stopped by the booth early on the second day and looked at the software briefly. He spent over five hours at my booth over the next two days, and even walked me to my truck when the expo was over. He was asking questions about everything except the software. "How do you find crews? How do you pay them? How do you find salesmen? How do you train them? How do you pay them?" And he asked many questions about the roofing process. He finally confessed that he'd bought a Stair, Door, and Trim company in Stroudsburg, Pennsylvania, and that a roofing company came with the deal. Then he said, "I don't know anything about roofing. I just wanted the other companies." When I asked him how many roofing jobs he was doing, his face lit up, "A little over five hundred roofs a year." I was speechless.

◆   ◆   ◆

The main reason that so many roofing companies start up and then go out of business in a year or two (or even a few months), is that the people starting them don't have a formula for success. Most often, the person starting the new roofing company has been a successful salesman, made some money, seen the profit margins, and decides he wants some of that action. But he doesn't have the first clue about *the business.* He knows a lot about sales, and a little about production, but he has never purchased advertising, insurance, paid employee taxes, been audited by his worker's comp carrier, or his liability insurance carrier, or the IRS, or paid for warranty issues, or forked over thousands of dollars to repair damage from a leak, or loaned a crew foreman thousands of dollars only to have him disappear, or the same for a salesman (or three, or ten). He simply knows nothing of *the business,* so he doesn't last long. I've heard that the number of those who actually make it may be as small as one in a hundred. That number wouldn't surprise me. The business isn't as simple as the typical roofing salesman believes. In fact, it's damned tough. My hat goes off to those who survive … but then again, they are the ones who need my help (and this book) the most.

The roofing business is fun ... sometimes. It is exciting ... sometimes, and you get the opportunity to help people ... sometimes. But I have never had anyone describe their reason for being in the roofing business by saying, "It is fun and exciting, and I really love helping people." We do it because there is a demand for it and because we can make money doing it.

Sometimes, if we do almost everything right, we can make a lot of money doing it. Sometimes, if we do almost everything right, we can lose our shirts. Likewise, either of those results can occur when we do almost everything wrong. It's a perplexing business.

A torrential rain can begin without warning when there was none in the forecast.

We can have crews sitting all day, afraid to work because the forecast called for heavy rains ... and not a drop falls.

The outside electrical outlet at a home doesn't work, and the crew doesn't have a generator. They weren't able to cut the ridge vent holes, but they installed the ridge vent anyway, hoping no one would notice. (That happened on one of my jobs. I didn't make it up.)

The crew didn't understand the difference between regular plywood and FRT, so they installed the plywood against the neighboring wall of the townhouse and installed the FRT out in the middle of the roof.

A customer calls the office the day after his job is done and says, "The crew did a wonderful job. They were really a great bunch. I love my new roof, but I've been asking around and I think you are charging me too much. I want a discount, or I'm not going to pay."

The supply company delivered the wrong color of shingles and the crew installed them.

The supply house couldn't deliver the shingles on time, so the crew had to pick them up, and then they read the address wrong and installed them on the wrong house.

The tires on the crew's truck missed the driveway and left big ruts in the yard.

The homeowner felt sorry for the crew because of the heat and gave them beer … before the job was finished. When he got home later, there were nine drunken roofers naked in his swimming pool. The attic was exposed, and there were heavy rains expected that night.

After one member of a crew removed a piece of rotten decking, another lost his balance and dropped a roll of felt through the hole. The home-owner called in a panic, "There's a big roll of something lying in the mid-dle of my bed." (That happened on the first job I ever sold in Virginia. I'm not making this stuff up.)

"They broke my favorite bush. I had it imported from Japan. It will cost four thousand dollars to get another one."

"That weather vane the crew broke was an antique. It's been in my fam-ily for many generations. It was priceless."

And my favorite one of all time happened on a job sold by a friend of mine in Virginia. The customer wouldn't pay, so Marty, the owner of the company, went out to visit with the customer. The following is the con-versation, as Marty related it to me afterward:

"Is there a problem with the job?"
"No, it's perfect. I love it."

"Then why won't you pay us?"

"I just don't want to."

"I'll put a lien on your house."

"I don't care. It's not my house. I just live here."

"You don't own the house! Then why did you sign the contract?"

"The house needed a roof. You're salesman never asked if I was the owner."

"I'll sue you personally."

"Get in line ... it's a long one."

"How about we go outside and I take the seventeen thousand out of your hide?"

"Okay, but then you'll be in jail, and I'm still not going to pay."

Welcome to the roofing business!

1

Setting The Table

Before we can get down to the specifics of how to rebuild and reorganize your roofing company, we need to get in the right mindset to do it. I'm ready if you are, so let's jump right in.

Take a Stand

The first step to long-term success in the roofing business is taking a stand and committing to it. You must decide what kind of company you want to build. Step back and think of yourself as a homeowner who needs a new roof. Ask yourself what kind of company you'd like to hire to do the job. And then become that kind of company.

Commit to becoming the kind of company who installs the best roofing system they can, who honors their commitments, who makes good on their word (written or verbal), and who cares about their customers, who cares about their salesmen, who cares about their crews, and who cares about their suppliers. Even though you fall short of perfection every day, wake up the next day with a renewed commitment to do better. Do that, and you are well on you way to making a lot of money in the roofing business.

Regardless of what kind of company you become though, you will not be right for every customer. People who are selling their homes may not be right for you. They may not care about quality. They may only be interested in the price. Wish them a happy life and move on.

Before you can hire the right kind of salesmen and ask them to represent you favorably; before you can expect your customers to put their trust in you; before you can establish your price; and before you train your crews; you must take a stand and commit to it. Lip service won't cut it. Where I'm from, we say, "That dog won't hunt".

What Business Are You In?

Don't try to be everything to everyone. Decide what business you're in, and then become good at it. If that is roofing, become the best roofing company you can be. If you want to do roofing and siding and gutters, then go for it. But become the best roofing company you can be. Become the best siding company you can be. And become the best gutter company you can be.

If you want to do roofing, siding, gutters, masonry work, windows, fences, railing, structural construction, patios, and decks, then stop calling yourself a roofing company. Throw this book away, and do some serious soul searching about who and what you are.

Of Mice and Men

We have entered the computer age. You can fight it, or deal with it. The choice is yours. If you fight it though, you will lose. It's as simple as that.

When I arrived at NVR in May of 2003, I found that they were using their computers as fancy typewriters, sparing them the use of whiteout. The owner didn't have one in his office. He didn't know how to use a mouse.

Today, John delights in hitting the intercom button and asking my wife, "Deryl, can you pull up the stats on Leesburg, Virginia and tell me my cost per sale on our Valpak advertising over the last six months?" She will have that information to him within minutes. John now communicates with many of his contacts via email, and he loves the number of leads generated by our new web site. He has become a dot com kinda guy! He knows what a search engine is, and he is constantly aware of our standing with the major ones. That didn't happen overnight, and it won't for you either.

NVR's 2003 re-roofing gross sales doubled in 2004, and doubled again in 2005, so let me say it again: We have entered the computer age. You can fight it, or deal with it. The choice is yours. If you fight it though, you will lose. It's as simple as that.

The Proper Balance

You have to balance your price with your cost and what your market will bear.

When I meet with a new client, whether it's for a short-term consulting job or a long term rebuilding effort, my first conversation with the owner is always the same. "Volume doesn't always equate to profit." And then I relate the story of my father's restaurant:

> It was a nice place, strategically located right in the split of the lanes of Route 66 in the Texas Panhandle. The dining room was almost always packed, but we didn't seem to be making any money. I knew very little about the restaurant business, so I didn't understand why. My father became very ill and I had to assume the role of manager on short notice and without much preparation. One of the first things I did was analyze the cost of serving every item on the menu. I found that we were actually losing money on half of the plates that went out of the kitchen. I printed up new menus immediately, making sure that we made a nice profit on each plate. When my father returned after several weeks, he got quite a surprise. "Where are all of the customers? What did you do?" I laughed and told him, "Dad, I cut the work in half and tripled the profits." When he looked at the books, he quickly got over the dining room not being packed.

Very few roofing companies do a cost analysis on a job prior to accepting the contract, and very few roofing salesmen do one prior to giving an estimate. Without computer software to help them, it is a very difficult thing to do cost analysis on the fly. Most often, the company will give their salesmen a general guideline, telling them to sell a 3-tab roof for X number of dollars per square, a thirty-year architectural shingle for X number of dollars per square, and so on. Then, the salesman is expected to take that base price and add the extras to it, things like steep pitch, removing extra layers, 2-story, cutting in new vents and such.

The devil is in the details though. GAF's Timbertex Hip & Ridge can cost $32.00 per bundle, while Elk's Seal-O-Ridge might cost as little as $21.00 per bundle. There are a host of other cost differences as well. Also, the salesman, especially if he is new, will often forget to allow for special circumstances on the roof, some of which are very costly. In other words, estimating a job in this manner is a shot in the dark at best. To compound matters, if the office doesn't do a cost analysis on the job prior to accepting it, the price deficiencies are not caught in advance of doing the job.

I will forego delving into how the advance cost analysis can be done easily and quickly until later. Let it suffice for now to say that not doing one is asking for trouble and is a major reason many companies do a large number of jobs at little or no profit.

Profit Margins

To understand the profit percentages being discussed in this book, you need to understand how I calculate them. I look at Gross Profit Percentage (GP%). When I use that term, I will be using the following formula: (Contract Price—Material Cost—Labor Cost)/Contract Price. Notice that I did not allow for Commissions, or Overrides, or Overhead. They will be dealt with separately. Stated another way, the GP% on the job is the percentage of the contract price that is left over after you pay for the materials and labor. This is not a typical accounting version of Gross Profit, but if we all understand what we mean by the term and we all calculate it the same way, there should be no confusion about what we are referring to and how we arrived at it.

> Ron Racehorse sold a roofing job for $10,000.00.
> We paid ABC Supply a total of $2,500.00 for the materials.
> We paid Pedro Martinez and his crew $3,500.00 for doing the job.
>
> $10,000.00–$2,500.00–$3,500.00 = $4,000.00 in Gross Profit
> $4,000.00/$10,000.00 = 40% (GP%)

The job made us a 40% Gross Profit.

Testing the Market

What price will your market allow? How much can you charge your potential customers and still close an acceptable number of the leads run? What do you consider an acceptable closing ratio? I can't answer those questions for you, but I can give you an educated opinion based on the wide variety of markets I've sold roofs in.

> *Note: I evaluate "Closing Ratios" based on the number of "Presentations Given", not on the number of leads run. If another company got there before me and already signed a contract with the customer, I do not count that against the closing ratio. Likewise, if the salesman gets to the home and discovers that the customer wants work done that we are not interested in doing (building an addition onto his house etc …), or isn't home and can't be contacted, that lead does not count against that salesman's closing ratio. I have different ways of tracking those outcomes, and I will discuss them later.*

I am told that the average closing ratio on presentations in the roofing industry nationwide is around 25%. I do not consider that to be acceptable, and I would not keep a salesman around long who could not do better than that, even in the markets with the most sophisticated and talented competition. The Washington, D.C. Metro area is one of those. The competition is intense, talented, and sophisticated. The potential client base is very educated, among the nation's highest income earners, and they are shoppers. They typically get three to ten estimates before making a buying decision. My salesmen average closing between 30% and 45% on presentations (after their first six months in the field). My personal closing ratio in that market fluctuated between 45% and 50% of presentations given.

In any market I go into, I do my market research starting at 40% Gross Profit. That is the minimum I will accept. I run a minimum of ten leads using that price guideline. After establishing my closing ratio at that price, I run another ten leads, basing my estimates on a 45% Gross Profit. I then compare my closing ratio on those estimates to those I gave based on the 40% Gross Profit. If my closing ratio dropped significantly, then I run another ten leads and base the estimate on 42 ½ % Gross Profit. Then, I compare that to my closing ratio at 40%. Doing this allows me to narrow in on the acceptable balance of Gross Profit to Closing Ratio for that market.

At NVR, my initial five new salesmen, hired in November of 2003 and the three hired in early 2004, averaged a Gross Profit Percentage of just over 42% in that highly competitive market for the year (2004). Of course, they were new and the competition was fierce. The following year (2005), the sales force as a whole, averaged just over 48% Gross Profit. They had figured it out.

In Stroudsburg, Pennsylvania in 2005, my closing ratio hovered between 75% and 80% on presentations given, with my price based on 42 ½% Gross Profit. Most customers told me later that mine was the highest estimate they received. In that market, the competition was less numerous and much less talented. The consumers were less sophisticated shoppers as well. I am told that the sales force that I hired and trained there, nearing the end of their first year at the time of this book, is averaging over 40% closing ratio and over 42% Gross Profit. They will get better over time.

My point is this: For the people who say, "Our market is different. You can't sell for those prices here, and you can't close that percentage of your presentations here." I say Poppycock! Or to put it more bluntly, Bullshit! Roofing is roofing, people are people, and sales are sales, regardless of what market you are in. Don't settle for less. You've already bought my book, so I have no reason to deceive you. It is what it is.

> *Note: I do my market research based on the number of sales made within two weeks of giving an estimate. My numbers, regardless of the market, average around 33%. The higher closing ratios come about over time, when customers who received estimates previously call in later and want to do business.*

Now, let me ask you again: What price will your market allow? How much can you charge your potential customers and still close an acceptable number of the leads run? What do you consider an acceptable closing ratio? Your answer should be 40+ GP% and something over 35% closing ratio, based on the number of presentations given. I'll teach you how to achieve at least that. Don't settle for less.

2

The Professional Roofing Office

The Outside

Why should you care about the outside of your roofing office? After all, very few customers will ever see it. In a large, highly populated market, most of your potential customers will never even drive by it, and if they do, they probably won't even notice.

How do you want your employees to feel about working for your company? Personally, I want them to be positive, happy, motivated, and proud to work for me. That applies to the office staff, the salesmen, the crews, the supplier reps, the manufacturer reps, and the mailman. It will be difficult, if not impossible, for them to start every workday happy, positive and motivated, if the first thing they see when they drive into the parking lot is a junk yard.

Keep the outside as clean as possible. If the building needs painting, paint it. If the sign bearing your company name is in ill repair, repair it, mend it, paint it, or whatever else it needs. If you have stacks (or more likely piles) of leftover shingles around, toss the worst of them and return the rest to the supplier for credit. Oh I can just hear you now. "That's a lot of money. We might use them someday." Yes it is a lot of money, but no, you will probably never use them. (Especially not for starter. You are not going to use old shingles for starter anymore, but that's a subject for a later chapter.) In any case, they are not worth the negative mental impact they have on everyone who drives into your parking lot. Get the place cleaned up!

The Inside

If you understand the importance of keeping the outside of your property clean, then I should be able to forego the lecture about keeping the inside clean ... so I will. Getting it organized and keeping it that way is another topic though, so I will spend some time on that.

The staff in most roofing company offices, whether the staff is one or ten, spends much of the day, if not most of it, searching for one thing or another. When an old customer calls with a leak (and can't even remember what year you did the job), or when a potential customer calls and wants to know why no one showed up to give him an estimate, the treasure hunt begins. Which crew did that job? What kind of shingles did we install? Which salesman was that lead given to? In a busy office, the next treasure hunt and the next and the next starts before the first one has been favorably concluded.

Most of the time, simply using the right computer software to track leads and job information will eliminate much of the searching, but not all of it. I have developed such a software package. I believe it's a good one, but I'm sure there are others that can accomplish the mission. You need to find one and use it.

Regardless of the size of your operation, your office needs **a computer system**—not just a computer or two—but a system. You need a **server** (with a backup system) that will be used to **network** the computers at each **workstation**, even the owner's. Yes, you need a computer too, and you need to learn how to use it. No really, you can do it. I know you're afraid, and that the mere mention of actually touching a mouse sends your anxiety level shooting off the scale. Just calm down, take a deep breath, and let it out slowly. Now, that's better. I'm sorry for scaring you like that, but you have to do it. Perhaps you can talk your nine-year-old into helping you master the basics.

Your computer network should be installed and maintained by a professional. With a little searching, you can find one who will take care of it for a reasonable price. You must get him to commit to helping you resolve computer related problems on short notice. Chris, our network guy at NVR, corrects problems remotely from his home. It's rare for a problem to be serious enough to cause him to drive the three hours to our office, but when that is necessary, he does it. You need to find someone like Chris.

Next, if you haven't already done so, you need to implement a **job numbering system.** Do not use the customer's name or address to identify the job. Every job should have a unique number that ties the information in the computer to the file containing the hard copies of paperwork generated on the job. Your suppliers must be instructed not to accept an order—not even from you—that doesn't have the job number prominently displayed on it.

> John Francis, the owner of NVR was the world's worst at violating this rule. We kept getting material bills from the various suppliers that had no job numbers on them. Almost every time, the material order bore John's name as the purchaser. Finally, I went into John's office and used his phone to call The Roof Center. When Cory, our rep, was on the phone, I hit the speaker button:
> "Cory, this is Neal at NVR. I have John sitting here with me and I have you on speaker." After the greetings were concluded, I continued, "The reason I'm calling is to serve you notice. The next time you accept an order from John Francis without a job number, NVR will stop ordering materials from The Roof Center. Are we clear?"
> There was an awkward moment of silence while John stared at me in disbelief. When my expression convinced him that I was serious, John put Cory out of his misery by saying, "It's okay, Cory, you heard him. I need to follow the rules like everyone else."

Your files should be arranged in the filing cabinet according to job number. They should be neat and all organized the same. I suggest buying folders with brads on both sides. Use a two-hole punch on every piece of paper that goes into the file. The contract should be on top, on the right side, with all of the supporting documents under it. Anything to do with money goes on the left side: material bills, labor bills, and copies of checks. It's a pain in the ass, but worth it.

Material bills that haven't yet been paid will be kept in a file for that supplier in the accounting office. However, once the bill has been paid, do not file it with all of the other material bills for that supplier. File it in the job file. I'm not sure why, but everyone has a problem with this at first, office staff and accountants alike. They get over it quickly, and it saves hundreds of hours of searching each year.

Likewise, **labor bills** are not to be filed in the crew's file. They are also to be filed with the job. Of course, that means that the crew must turn in a separate invoice on each job … as they should anyway.

You should have an **intercom system**, even if you only have a two or three-room office. I personally prefer an intercom system that is independent from the telephone and one that transmits to every receiver in the office. If you have a tool room and/or warehouse, put units there too. That way, the user doesn't have to know who is in which room to page them. Radio Shack sells the perfect system. It's inexpensive and it works well. (I think the cost is about $25–$30 per unit.) Each unit simply plugs into an electrical outlet and uses the office wiring to carry the message. There is no additional wiring required. It is important that the person being paged acknowledge that they heard the page, so that the sender doesn't have to wonder about it. A simple "Thank you" will suffice.

Poison

At some point during the nine years that my family owned and operated the restaurant in Texas on Route 66, my frustration about salaries reached a peak. "Why does Linda make ten cents more per hour than me? Or, "A little bird told me that Susan makes more than I do. If that's true, we have a big problem." And on, and on, and on, and on.

> I was attending West Texas State University at the time and my major was Psychology. I was older than most of the other students, not having started college until after military service, getting married, and having two children. I related more to the professors than to the other

students, so I would often lunch at their table in the cafeteria. They were all practicing psychologists as well as teachers, so I posed the problem to them. "How can I stop all of the bickering about how much everyone is getting paid?"

After thinking about it for a moment, Dr. Byrd asked me, "Neal, how do you decide how much to pay each of them? Do you base it on skill, experience, length of service, reliability, job performance, how much you like them, or the size of their boobs?"

Of course, I answered that I considered all of those things … except for the last two. (Okay, so I lied a little.) Dr. Byrd nodded and then told me how to solve my problem. He told me to go back to my restaurant, take out a pen and paper, and list out all of the good points about each employee on a separate sheet. Next, I was to list out all of the bad points on each one and things they needed to improve on. "Then, evaluate those lists and see if you are paying them fairly. If you are not, then you need to adjust their pay accordingly. However, if you are paying them fairly, then type up a list of their names with their salaries beside it. Post that list in their work area and then wait for them to come complaining to you. As each one comes in, go over their list with them and let them know what they need to improve on to get a raise. You might say, 'When someone calls in sick at five in the morning, I know I can call Linda and she will come in and help me out of a jam. You never answer your phone, or if you do, you always have an excuse why you can't come in.' There are probably hundreds of things like that which make one employee more or less valuable to you than another one."

Dr. Byrd ended the conversation by saying, "Neal, secrets are poison to any work environment. Avoid them at every opportunity."

I did exactly what Dr. Byrd had suggested … and it worked. It also opened my eyes to my own method of passing out raises.

Sometimes it's difficult, but you should avoid letting situations develop which necessitate keeping something secret around the office. If you pay your brother's daughter more than you pay someone else, just be honest about it. "I pay her more because she's my niece. It's a family thing. Get over it."

Elvis Is In The Building

What is the purpose of a roofing office? The roofing business is about sales and production. The office is simply a place to coordinate and support those activities. When a salesman walks through the front door, he should be welcomed with bright, cheery smiles and genuinely warm greetings. Crew foremen and their workers should receive exactly the same treatment. Without salesmen and crews, the office staff would be unemployed … and so would you. No one should ever be too busy to smile and greet a salesman or crew member. If you're on the phone, ask the person on the other end of the line to please hang on a second, then smile and greet your salesman or crew member.

On the flip side, salesmen and crew members should respect the office staff. They should treat them as vital, and let them know daily how much they are appreciated. Please. Thank you. If it wouldn't be too much trouble …? Is it possible that you can do …? Would you mind doing …? All should be prerequisites to asking an office staff member to do something, even if that thing is exactly what that office staff member was hired to do. You are no different. You should follow those same guidelines of common decency and respect.

The Gatekeeper

A roofing company's receptionist is as important as anyone in the company, if not more so. She is first in line to answer the phone, take leads, calm irate customers, and direct calls to the other departments. She should be hired based on five criteria: Personality, personality, organization skills, personality, and personality.

NVR is lucky. Kay has been sitting at the same desk for over 20 years, and for a very good reason … personality. By the time an irate customer gets transferred to the production department, to the sales manager, to the accounting department, or to the owner, she already has them calmed down … if not laughing. I have heard her take 30 leads in rapid succession, with the 30th receiving the same happy, cheery greeting as the first. She only has a couple of thousand other responsibilities, not the least of which is doing whatever she is asked to do, whether it's her job or not. But she never shows her frustration, her weariness, or her anger, even when you know it has to be in there somewhere.

Stroudsburg Roofing is lucky too. Kathy, even though tripling as office manager, production manager, and receptionist (and a few other things), somehow manages to brighten every caller's day. I've seen her lose it, but it doesn't happen very often, and never until after she has hung up the phone.

In both of those companies, potential customers are well on their way to being sold before their initial call has ended. I can't tell you how many customers I've had mention their initial call to the office and what a pleasant experience it was, especially after calling two or three other companies. I have sometimes gotten the feeling that a customer signed up with me just to keep from letting Kay or Kathy down.

You would be well served to find someone like that to handle your front office.

The Hot Seat

To explain the workings of the Production Department would require a separate book, much longer than this one. I do, however, feel the need to give you a few basic guidelines.

First, design and install a board in the production office that displays each job, its status, the supply company where the materials were ordered, the projected delivery date, the crew that is doing the job, and the salesman who sold it. Develop a system for how the production board is updated and maintained.

Salesmen and office staff should know the system, be able to look at the board and answer questions about the status of a job when the need arises … without having to ask the Production Manager. However, no one other than the Production Manager should change or update the board. I have a system that works, with cards placed in slots that are moved from one stage to the other, with notes made on them in specific places. But I've seen other systems that work too.

Next, train your Production Manager, and then stay the hell out of that office. Never pass out a job, order the materials for a job, agree to pay a crew more for something, or promise to have a particular job completed on a certain day. Answer every such request with, "I'll have to check with my Production Manager, but I'll see what I can do for you."

Salesmen should never promise the customer that their job will be done on a specific day. They should answer every such request with, "I'll have to check with our Production Manager, but I'll see what I can do."

The Production Manager should notify the customer and the salesman when the materials are scheduled for delivery, and when the job is passed to the crew for installation.

If changes are made to the job via a call from the customer to the Production Manager, the salesman should be notified immediately. The salesman should provide the first line of Quality Control and Customer Relations. That is always difficult, but it is impossible if the salesman is taken out of the loop at any phase of the process.

> Note: I will address the salesman's responsibilities at length in a later chapter.

Finally, if you manage to find a good Production Manager, hit your knees every night and thank the god of your choice. I have sat in the hot seat more times than I care to remember. I'm not very good at it, but I have had the privilege to know some good production managers ... and three great ones. First and foremost is Deryl, my wife. She hates doing it, but there is no one better. The other two are Crystal W. and Rob W. (not related). They know who they are, and my hat goes off to them.

Staff Size

Unfortunately, I can't tell you how many people you'll need in your office. Each company is different. You have to evaluate the nature of your business and decide what is right for you based on your particular situation. But don't staff your office according to the volume of business you're doing. Staff it according to the volume of business you should be doing, or the volume you want to be doing in the near future.

Jimmy Yoo came to this country from Korea without a dime to his name. He is one of the most successful businessmen I've ever had the privilege to work for. At the time I left his employ, he owned several banks, a sign company, and several other businesses. I was the office manager for his sign company, which was the business that had garnered him the money to buy all of his other holdings.

One day, Jimmy told me that I should put an ad in the paper for a new person to work in his sign factory. "Why, who are we losing?"

He replied with a grin, "No one. I want to add one."

"But we're barely keeping the ones we've got busy. Sales have been down."

Jimmy laughed, put his hand on my shoulder and said, "We need to get sales up, especially now that we're going to have an additional man in the factory." Then he got more serious. He looked me in the eye and said, "If you wait until you've got the business, you won't have time to train a new man. You'll have mad customers because we're not getting signs out of the factory fast enough. You should hire and train the number of people you'll need to handle the volume you want to be doing six months from now. Never build a new highway to handle the volume it will get today. By the time you get the thing finished, it won't be able to handle the load."

A footnote to that little story: Many years after leaving Jimmy Yoo's employ (on good terms), I was in Oshkosh, Wisconsin and had just opened my own roofing company. The foreman of a siding crew came in looking for work for his crew. His last name was Yoo. I mentioned that I had once worked for a man by that name in Dallas. "Jimmy Yoo?" the crew foreman asked, with awe in his voice. I answered yes and then asked him if they were related. He explained that he was a distant relative, but that he'd never met Jimmy. Then he went on to explain that Jimmy Yoo was considered something of a God, or at least a hero throughout the Korean community all over the U.S.A. He shook my hand earnestly and told me what a great honor and privilege it would be to work for someone who actually knew Jimmy Yoo personally.

Cross Training

We all think cross training is a great idea, but we don't get around to it as often as we should, or to the extent we should, especially in a busy office. I often hear: "I'm swamped with my job and she's swamped with hers, and it's just easier and quicker to do it myself."

If you have a general manager, or an office manager, they should be able to fill in for any member of the staff without losing a beat. If you don't have one of those, then you should be able to do every job in the office yourself. The beauty of having a "system" is that it makes filling in for someone easier. If you've let your production manager or other staff members come up with their own system, then filling in for them is a nightmare.

McLean, Texas, 1978. Donna, my morning shift cook in the restaurant was a partier and heavy drinker. It wasn't unusual for her to be late or not show up at all. I let it go on because I couldn't do her job. Deryl was a great cook and would usually fill in for her for an hour or two, or the entire shift if Donna didn't show.

One morning, it came to a head. At fifteen minutes past the time when Donna should have been at work, I called her. She was asleep and told me, "I'll be there in a couple of hours." I got mad. "If you're not here in fifteen minutes, don't bother coming in ... ever." And I hung up the phone.

The phone rang a minute or two later, but I was back in the kitchen trying to get the grills turned on and getting as much done as I knew how to do. One of the waitresses came back to the kitchen and told me, "Donna called. She'll be here in thirty or forty-five minutes." I had already made up my mind though. "I told her if she's not here in fifteen minutes, she's fired ... and I meant it. That was five minutes ago, so she only has ten minutes left."

That day, I became a cook. I was determined never to let myself get in that situation again. I never got very good at cooking, but that wasn't the point. The point was that finally, everyone knew that I could do their job, and that I wasn't opposed to doing it.

If you have one person in your office who is the only one that knows a job, that person has you over a barrel. Don't let that situation develop. If it already exists, do something about it immediately.

By the Book

I'm an old military man. The chain of command is never violated … at least not without serious consequences. Don't violate it. Give your managers the authority they need to accomplish their mission, and then never allow anyone to go over their heads to you without first going to them.

Neither John Francis nor Seth Peyser ever mastered this simple concept. They both tried, and bless them for making the effort, but they never succeeded. They violated the chain of command every day, sometimes several times a day. It's not easy. You're the boss and you're used to micromanaging everything. But the degree to which you can master the chain of command, is the degree to which you will enable your managers to become successful.

The first step in mastering and properly using the chain of command is letting your managers know that you really want to do it. Give them permission to scold you when you violate it. Insure that they know that you are trying and that you need their help to master it.

> I was riding in the car with John when a salesman called him. I could tell from his end of the conversation that it was something that the salesman should have called me about. I tapped John on the shoulder and said, "Tell him to call me, and then hang up." He did, but I could tell that it was very difficult for him to relinquish that control. He never did master it, but he tried.

> Seth Peyser came to me and began relating to me a conversation that he'd had with one of my people. "Neal, I was talking to George about his pay and I think we may have a problem. I think—"
> "Seth, stop right there. What were you doing talking to George?"
> "He came to me and—"

"Damnit, Seth. George has no business coming to you about anything. Why didn't you shut him down and tell him that he needs to
come to me?"

"I … he came to me and … you're right."

Don't do that to your managers. Handcuff your ego to your bed before
getting out of it in the morning. Let your managers manage. And don't
call them on the carpet for making a mistake on a particular job, or making a decision that you don't agree with. Hold them accountable for the
sum total of their accomplishment. They will screw up everyday, just like
you would if you were doing their job. Get on them when they screw up
too much. When you do call them on the carpet though, don't mention
one specific incident or job. Talk about their overall performance, both
good and bad.

"Bob, I'm hearing too many complaints from customers about their not
being notified when their job is starting."

"Oh, like who? Can you be more specific?"

"I can, but I'd rather not. I don't want us to get bogged down in the
specifics of one job. There's been a lot of smoke lately about it though, so I
have to assume that there's at least a little fire causing it. Some of them are
probably full of shit, but there have been too many to ignore. I'm going to
be paying a little more attention to that, and I want you to make a con-
certed effort to improve on it."

Once you allow yourself to get caught up in the specifics of one job or
one problem, you're sunk. Don't fall into that trap. Again, hold your managers accountable for their overall performance, not their mistakes or
faulty judgment on one job or one situation.

Never correct or override or downgrade your manager or his decisions
in front of others—not other managers, other office staff, and for sure, not
their subordinates. Here's an answer that you will find useful when faced
with having to make a comment about a manager's decision. "Well, you
and I weren't privy to every conversation or circumstance along the way.

I'm sure that he had a good reason for doing what he did, based on the facts presented to him at the time." And then change the subject.

3

The Professional Roofing Salesman

Many years ago, I happened to notice a copy of *Business Week* magazine lying on the coffee table in an advertising office waiting room (at least I think it was *Business Week,* but my memory has faded). The picture on the cover and the headline caught my eye. The picture was of a very handsome, sharply dressed, professional looking man. The headline said something like: "Your best salesman … love him, hate him." I had some time, so I sat down and read the four or five-page article.

I don't really remember much of what was in the article, but I do remember the point it made. The typical Racehorse or Stud salesman is an arrogant asshole. He has a very high opinion of himself, and a very low opinion of everyone else, especially the people who work in the office. He is above the rules and doesn't hide his disdain for being asked to comply with them. He is a god, and everyone else is there to serve him. He doesn't seem to notice that everyone hates him, but if he did know, he wouldn't care. He is a master at manipulation. He manipulates everyone and everything around him. The article concluded with something to the effect that: "Now, wouldn't it be great if we could hire ten more just like him."

I have worked with and around a few Racehorses and Studs. I don't like them and I refuse to have one of them on my sales team. I don't care how much they can sell. I would rather have a young, clean-cut, well-mannered guy who respects others and the rules, and who cares about his customers and the company he works for.

Remove the Blindfold

If I took you into a room, handed you some darts, blindfolded you, spun you around a few times, and told you to hit the bull's eye on the dartboard, you'd probably miss. It sounds silly to even try, yet that is very similar to the approach most companies take when hiring salesmen. They start throwing the darts before they've developed a clear view of the target. Oh sure, they have a general idea of what they want and what they will expect of a new hire, but nothing really specific. Let's remove the blindfold and focus.

I have grown weary of trying to teach old dogs new tricks, only to have them revert back to their old ways the first time my way becomes uncomfortable or doesn't work for them. I have had a great deal of success hiring people from outside the roofing and construction industries and training them from scratch. I greatly prefer going that route. The less they know about roofing and construction, the more appealing they are to me. I suggest that you develop the same mindset.

Basic Qualifications

1. I will expect a salesman to dress neatly, slacks and a nice looking shirt, and be well groomed.

2. He will need to be somewhat intelligent to absorb the massive amount of information that I will dump on him over a very short time.

3. He will need to be articulate.

4. He should be outgoing. He can't be shy, reserved, or an introvert.

5. He should exude confidence, but not arrogance.

6. He should be believable and appear honest and sincere.

7. He should be respectful of others and well mannered.

8. He should be reasonably fit. He will have to carry and climb a ladder and walk on roofs.

9. He can't be overly afraid of heights.

10. He should have passable reading and writing skills.

11. He should have some basic computer skills, the more the better.

12. He should be free of oddities in appearance or personality that might distract from what he is saying, or which might cause people to be put off by him before they have a chance to get to know him. (Examples: I am personally put off by visible body and facial piercings. I am also put off by someone who is overtly "flaming" gay. I don't care if he is gay, so long as he's not blatantly obvious about it. Likewise, I am put off by bad breath or rancid body odors).

13. He should have a valid driver's license.

14. He should be free of addictions to alcohol or drugs to any extent that will affect his work. If he has such addictions, he should be in recovery and a member of some recovery support group (AA, NA or the like.)

15. He should avoid vulgarities, or at least exercise good judgment in their use. (Hopefully better than me.)

16. He should own a vehicle capable of carrying a 28' ladder and a few roofing materials, or be willing to trade into one within a reasonable length of time.

17. Lastly, he should not be an avid member of any religion that prohibits him from working on Saturdays. Saturday is the best selling day of the week because that is when most people are home during the day. Also, our crews work on Saturday and he will need to check in on his jobs in progress.

I can just hear you now. "My Gawd! How are we ever going to find several candidates who meet those qualifications?" For now, I'm going to use those dreaded words, "Trust me." They are out there and I'm going to tell you not only how to find them, but how to interview and hire them. However, there are some other things we must do first.

Before we can advertise for and interview a candidate, we must first decide what we are hiring him to do. As you will see from the Job Description listed below, my salesmen are more than salesmen … a lot more.

Job Description

1. After training, we are going to ask him to run leads. I have found that three leads per day is the optimum number, given the other responsibilities he will be given. (Sometimes, even three is too many.)

2. I insist that my salesmen be punctual. If their appointment is set for 10:00 a.m. and they show up at exactly 10:00 a.m., they are ten minutes late.

3. I insist that my salesmen get up on a potential customer's roof to inspect and measure it. (Except in situations where doing so would prove too dangerous). I will explain my reasons for that in the section about the sales presentation.

4. I use a two-call close and I will expect him to do the same. I do not like smooth-talking, slick, hard-closers. I won't buy from them, so how can I expect my customers to?

5. When he turns in a new job, I will expect him to also turn in a Material Order, a Labor Order, a detailed Job Cost Analysis with the contract, and a deposit check for at least one third of the contract price.

6. I will expect him to make at least one trip (preferably two) to the job site while the job is in progress (for quality control and customer relations).

7. If he has short-measured the roof, or left needed materials off of the Material Order, I will expect him to go to the supply company for

them, and take them to the job site. It was his mistake, so he should suffer the consequences. Making mistakes should cost something, otherwise what motivation does he have for being more careful?

8. If he has drastically long-measured the roof, I will expect him to return the leftover materials to the supply company for credit. Again, it was his mistake.

9. I will expect him to inspect the job after it is completed and collect the final payment.

10. If there are deficiencies in workmanship, I will expect him to notify the production department and provide them with a detailed Work Order for the corrections.

11. I will expect him to get involved, if necessary, should there be any problems or complaints about the job, during, or after completion, and any warranty issues later. (They are still *his* customers and he should have the best rapport with them.)

12. I will expect him to attend regular sales meetings and special training classes.

13. I will expect him to provide the office with accurate (and brutally honest) feedback on the status and final disposition of each and every lead he is given.

14. When leads are slow, I will expect him to be imaginative in developing new marketing strategies, and be willing to help implement them.

15. I will expect him to take a proactive approach to researching and learning about new products and installation techniques.

16. I will expect him to make himself available to assist other salesmen when his schedule permits. We are a team.

17. I will expect him to work most Saturdays, and do catch-up work on Sundays, if necessary. I am always amazed at how many "religious"

people are shocked when we mention working on Sunday. But they would be the first to scream bloody murder if their electricity didn't work on Sunday, or the gas station or restaurant wasn't open, or they couldn't watch their favorite football team because the TV people didn't work on Sunday. We will do what we have to do to become successful.

18. I will expect him to take care of the company tools and equipment issued to him and replace what he breaks.

19. Lastly, I will expect him to answer his phone, 24–7, 365, just as I do. (I once had a customer call while I was in the shower. I stepped out and answered it, explaining to him that I would have to call him back because I was in the middle of my shower. "You were in the shower and still answered your phone?" I replied, "I can't help it. It's a habit.")

Again, I can hear you mumbling, "No roofing salesman is going to agree to do all of that." Exactly, that's why I don't hire experienced roofing salesmen. So far, I have not had trouble hiring qualified candidates from outside the roofing and construction industries, and getting them to agree to do the things listed above. They don't know that I'm asking a lot of them. And besides, when they hear about the potential reward for becoming successful at it, they would have agreed to stand on their head during training. So, let's talk about how and how much we're willing to pay them.

Employee vs. Sub-Contractor

More than any other industry I know, the roofing industry (or at least the residential re-roofing industry) has developed a mindset that everyone other than office staff should be a sub-contractor. I worked on that basis during my first four years in the business. I have hired salesmen on that basis … a lot of them. There is only one problem—no, there are many problems with doing it that way, not the least of which is that it is illegal.

I am going to forego listing out the famous ten questions that the ⅃ lists as the general guideline for distinguishing between an employee and a sub-contractor. If you haven't seen the list, go to the IRS website (or get your nine-year-old to go there for you) and print out the list. However, don't make the mistake that others, including myself, have made. Don't rationalize your way around the various questions on the list. The fact is, even if you can answer all of the questions in a way that makes your guy look like a sub-contractor, that doesn't mean that he really is … legally.

> A brief example: One company I worked for had a good roofing crew. They worked for the company for several years. During an audit by the IRS, the auditor told us that the crew was not a sub-contractor, but an employee. We argued that he qualified as a sub-contractor according to the ten questions. However, when the auditor checked the crew's personal financial records, they found that he had not done work for, or been paid by any other company during those years. "But he was free to do so. We didn't forbid it," we argued. "It was his choice." The auditor didn't care. They changed his status to employee and made us pay the back employee taxes on him for the entire several years that he had worked for the company.

But let's be realistic. We have never found a way to make roofing crews employees and still make a profit—at least not in the residential re-roofing side of the business. Worker's Compensation Insurance, Liability Insurance, Taxes, and having to pay them during down time, all make it difficult, if not impossible. So I'm not suggesting that you make your crews employees. I don't know how to do it and still make a decent profit (at least not without charging the customers so much that I'm never able to sell a job).

Salesmen are different though. They don't get paid as much as an entire roofing crew. And, as you saw in the Job Description listed above, I'm going to control them to an extent, and require things of them that make it impossible to pass them off as sub-contractors. The office is even going to set their appointments for them. Yes, you understood me correctly. We're going to require that they be in a certain place at a certain time and do certain things while they are there. That, in and of itself, disqualifies them as sub-contractors. Deal with it.

Commissions

My first year as a salesman, I was paid 10% of every dollar I brought into the office—not on what I sold—but what I collected. My second year, my commission was raised to 13%, also based on collections. My fourth year, Marty came up with something new, a Percentage of Profit commission formula. He would advance me money on each job as it was collected. Then, after the job was "capped out" and all of the material and labor bills had been received by the office, the profit was calculated. He then gave me more money, or took some back, depending on the differential between what he had already paid me on the job and what I had actually earned on the job. That year, I averaged 17 ½% commissions on my total gross sales.

I believe that 13% is a fair commission in a non-storm-chasing company. Permanent roofing companies have a much higher overhead. So, when I got to NVR and hired my new salesmen, I structured their pay in such a way that I thought they would earn around 13%. It didn't work out that way though. At the end of the first year, we discovered that we had only paid them (as a group) a little under 12%. That dropped to 10.8% their second year. Why? They had sold more than I had initially expected. Don't you just hate it when that happens?

The Dreaded Salary

What keeps many very qualified candidates from accepting a sales position in any industry? The number one answer is Straight Commissions. Let's face the facts. We are asking a very sharp, intelligent young man to go to work in a new industry, learn a new skill, work from can until can't, use his own vehicle, and burn his own gas … and with no guaranteed income. That is a very scary thing for anyone.

Paying salesmen a salary went against everything I believed. I thought it was a crazy thing to do. But after thinking back to the many new salesmen I'd hired over the years, something jumped out at me: Draws. I had always been fairly liberal with giving new salesmen draws against future commissions … just to get them by until they were trained and got their pipeline full. After all, I didn't want them to starve or lose their vehicles, or be evicted from their homes, or not have money for gas to run their leads. It dawned on me then that I was indeed paying them a salary. I just wasn't reaping the benefits of doing so. They were still sub-contractors, so I couldn't control them like I wanted to.

Finally, I decided to give the salary thing a try. I would set their salary at an amount that I would otherwise have given them in draws. Then, since I wasn't going to deduct the salary from their future commissions, I would lower their commission percentage enough to allow me to recoup that money. All I had to do was estimate how much they would sell, do the math, and come up with a commission percentage that would make their total compensation come out to 13% of their gross sales. So that's what I did.

While doing these calculations, I kept one thing firmly in mind. I did not want to pay them enough salary to make them "comfortable" or "satisfied". I believe that commissions motivate, and salary subdues. I wanted them to stay hungry and eager, with their eyes constantly on the carrot.

But like I said earlier, they sold more than I had estimated, so their salaries worked out to a lesser percentage than I had calculated. Therefore, their total compensation was less than 13% (even with bonuses and prizes they received from sales contests). They didn't complain though. They were making more money than they ever dreamed possible, so they were happy. Damn! I decided not to open up that can of worms, so I just left things the way they were.

The salary I had settled on was $25,000 per year. I set their commission at 10%, based on collections. I didn't want them to come back later and ask for things like gas money, and money for supplies though, so I told them up front that the salary was intended to cover those things.

John the Genius

During the interview process with my first five new salesmen (whom I later nicknamed The A-Team), the last step was taking them in to meet John. I did that more for their benefit than for his. But this whole thing was an experiment, and he was going to be laying out a lot of money up front (you'll understand that better when I explain how I equipped them), so I wanted to keep John involved in the process.

Two of those I took in to meet John blindsided me at the last minute. They wanted more salary. They hadn't mentioned anything about it to me prior to sitting down with John. One wanted $30,000 and the other asked for $35,000. Both made it clear that not giving them the higher salary was a deal-breaker. I was stunned, but like I said earlier, they were sharp, intelligent guys, so I guess I should have expected some negotiation.

The first of the two was Ryan. He was, at the time, an area food representative for Sysco Foods. He was Vietnamese, and spoke fluently in that language, plus Chinese and English. The D.C. Metro area has a huge Asian population, so we knew that would work to his advantage. His appearance, body language, attitude, confidence and manner, gave us little doubt that he would be great at whatever occupation he chose. He was a stud, a racehorse, but not in all of the negative ways that I mentioned earlier.

When Ryan demanded the higher salary, John grinned and scratched his chin. I could see his brain working. Finally, he winked at me and then told Ryan, "Okay, but you'll have to settle for 8% commission instead of 10%. Then, we'll give you 90 days after training to revert back to the $25,000 and 10% commission. It will be your choice, but we'll only give you 90 days to make your decision." Ryan accepted those terms. He was in my office 8 days after training asking for his salary to be lowered to $25,000 and his commission percentage raised to 10%. Like I said, he was a sharp guy.

The second of the two was Eric. John made him the same deal. It took Eric a little longer to realize the mistake he'd made. In fact, it took him almost three weeks after training to request the lower salary and higher commission percentage. We teased him about being so slow to figure it out.

4

Find Them, Hire Them

Commitment

I try to commit to everything I do, or not do it. But there are different levels of commitment. Some people like to get "involved" in things without becoming "committed" to them. I'm not that way—not about many things. I don't like salesmen who "just want to stick their toe in the water to see what it's like." My way may not be the right way, but my way is to jump in headfirst and figure out how to swim later.

I once heard someone describe the difference between being involved and being committed this way: Think of your normal breakfast, a plate of ham and eggs. The chicken was involved but the pig was committed. I think that pretty much sums up my feelings on commitment. I like people who aren't afraid to commit.

The Right Stuff

A father sent his son off to one of the best universities in the country. When his son returned, the father was not happy with the results. He called the dean of the university and said, "I sent you my son, and you sent me back an educated idiot." The dean replied, "Sir, we can only educate what you send us."

"You can't make a silk purse out of a sow's ear." Building a quality sales team begins with finding quality people. I have never had much luck finding quality sales applicants from advertising in the newspaper. (There have been exceptions, but not many.) I've gotten hundreds (if not thousands) of responses, conducted dozens and dozens of interviews, and hired a lot of them. None can compare to the quality of those I found on Monster.com.

Advertising on Monster.com was a last minute decision. I wanted applicants to have some basic computer skills, so it only made sense to float a job posting over the Internet and see what would happen. I figured that an applicant would have to know how to use a computer to see the ad. I was, however, not optimistic about the results. Obviously, I was very pleasantly surprised.

The ad that I posted on Monster.com was fairly simple, but it had some unique elements. If I remember correctly, I set the first year income at $55K-$150K. I gave a brief description of the company, but I didn't go into much about the actual nature of the work. I did make a bulleted list of what qualifications I wanted, and another one of what applicants could expect from us. Things like Base Salary, Generous Commission Package, Leads, No Cold Calling, and that kind of thing. Regarding the qualifications part of the ad, our Monster.com representative told me that I had been rather blunt and harsh. I had, but I didn't want wimps to apply. I wanted confident guys who weren't afraid of hard work and straight talk.

The unique part of the ad was the way I explained that I didn't want to see resumes. I just wanted applicants to send me a personal note, telling me as much about themselves as they felt comfortable sharing. Then, I instructed our Monster.com representative to disable all of the automatic response buttons on the ad. I didn't want an applicant to be able to simply click a button to send me a resume and stock cover letter. Many found a way to do that anyway. Obviously, those applicants couldn't follow simple instructions, so I tossed them in the trash. I also trashed the ones who couldn't string words together in a meaningful way, and those who lived too far away.

When I received a personal note from someone who seemed interesting, I would fire back a letter explaining more about the position. The letter emphasized the negative aspects of being a roofing salesman every bit as much as it did the positive aspects. The letter ended with an invitation to call our office to schedule an interview—"If you're still interested." I like doing that. I like getting the negative things about the job (and there are a lot of them) out on the table right up front. I don't want any applicant to tell me later, "You painted too rosy a picture."

When an applicant called the office, I would not speak with them. Our receptionist would simply schedule the appointment. I didn't want to get sucked in to conducting phone interviews.

The Interview

After giving an applicant time to tell me (or sell me) about himself, and after asking him a few basic questions, I will give him a brief rundown on our company, its history, the owner, and me. Sometimes I will get long-winded (as I'm sure you've already discovered), but I try my best to keep that part brief.

Sometime prior to their eyes glazing over, I will begin what I consider to be most important statements that I will make during the interview. I will almost always start with:

"Jeremiah, I wish I could sit here and tell you that we've got this whole thing figured out, that we've got the perfect system in place and we'd like to plug you into it. The system can't fail. Every play in our playbook is designed to go for a touchdown. I guarantee it." (I stole that line from Art Williams, one of the most effective recruiters I've ever listened to. In fact, I've stolen a lot of what I do from him. He's worth stealing from. If you've never heard him speak, you've missed out on something very, very special.)

I will continue with: "But unfortunately, I can't look you in the eye and tell you that—not and keep a straight face. The fact is that, until a short time ago, this company was just another roofing company. We decided to change. The owner and I have made a commitment—a strong commitment—to change the way we do business. We want to become better, more professional. We want to take this company to a new level of professionalism. That's why you're sitting here today. We need people like you to help us do that. We'll do it, with or without you. We're going to do it … or die trying. We have a plan, a vision for what the finished product is going to look like, but that plan is still a work in progress. It will be tweaked and modified and altered a thousand times before we get it right.

That will be frustrating for you. You'll get frustrated and pissed off about something every day, especially when we change things around on you. But we'll only do that when we're convinced that the changes will make things better for you and for us. The bottom line is this: We are committed to becoming the best, most professional, most reliable, most trustworthy company in this market. And we are committed to having the most highly trained, most dedicated, most professional sales force in the industry … bar none."

By this time, if I'm still sitting down, then I'm not at my best. I believe what I'm saying, and I want him to see that I believe it. It's not unusual for me to be pacing around the office, banging my hand on the desk, or waving my arms in the air. I don't fake that. I believe it and I'm excited about it. And I want my excitement to infect him.

"We've designed a method of doing roofs that's better than any company in this market—hell—better than any company in the country is doing them. We're going to equip you with a laptop, a printer, and a digital camera … all hooked up in your vehicle so you can use them right there in the customer's driveway. Very few other roofing salesmen in the world have all of those things, if any. We're going to give you the best damn training in the industry, and the most sophisticated roofing estimate software in the world. The only way you'll be able to keep from reaching the end zone is if you trip on your own feet or drop the friggin ball. And we're going to make sure that you never have to worry about paying your rent again. We want you to make money … a lot of money. The owner of this company loves signing big commission checks … the bigger the better. The only way he'll make money is if you make money."

At some point I'll stop and look him right in the eyes and say something like, "Sorry, but I get a little excited just thinking about it. So … how does all of this sound to you so far?"

Then, I throw cold water on the whole thing. "Okay, now let's talk about the other side of it, the part about how exhausted you're going to get, how frustrated, how pissed off, how dejected and down in the mouth you're going to get. This is a very difficult job. Not everyone is cut out for it. You'll have to grow some pretty thick skin. Your customers are going to bitch at you. The office is going to bitch at you. The crews are going to bitch at you. I'm going to bitch at you. Your wife is going to bitch at you for never being home, for working all the time, for being too tired to pay her any attention when you get home, and for not making a zillion dollars in the first month. You're going to come to me and stare at the floor and whine, and tell me that you just don't know if you're cut out for it. You'll want me to hug you and pat you on the back and sympathize with you. But I'll probably give you a swift kick in the ass and tease you for thinking that it's supposed to be easy to earn a hundred or a hundred and fifty, or two hundred thousand dollars in a year. Jeremiah, if you think this is an easy job, you're sadly mistaken. It's tough as hell. If it were easy, there would be a line of men outside my door begging to do it for thirty-five or forty thousand a year. We wouldn't need you ... and we damn sure wouldn't be willing to pay you what we're willing to pay you for doing it."

Before I conclude the interview by telling them about the salary and commission structure, I usually steal a little—no, a lot more—from Art Williams: "Jeremiah, I don't know if you can do this. There is no test devised that can look inside the heart of a man or woman and tell if they've got the goodies or not. All I can do is trust my gut and make my best guess about you. I don't want to be one of those guys who just throws a pile of shit against the wall and hope that some of it sticks. If you decide to trust me and come on board, I promise that I'll do everything in my power to see that you succeed. But I can't do it for you. Whether you make it or not will be up to you ... whether you've got the goodies inside you or not."

And then I do my best to paint them a picture of the dream. (Sorry, but it's another bit of Art's recruiting method that works ... if it's true, and if you sincerely believe it. I do.) "Now, what's the payoff? What's in the pot at the end of the rainbow? Well, I'm going to tell you. It's learning a set of skills that will make you money for the rest of your life—a lot of money—by doing something that you can feel good about, in a way that you can feel good about it, a way that won't keep you up at night with a guilty conscience. If you learn this thing, you'll have a sense of freedom, because no one will ever be able to put their thumb on you again. I hate to put it in these terms, but if I came to work tomorrow morning and this place was on fire, and the owner's body was out in the parking lot smoldering with the paramedics trying to put the fire out on him so they could put him in the body bag, I'd feel very bad for him and his family and all of the people who work here. But if I wanted to, I could have another job, earning six figures before the sun went down. That's what I hope to give you. Every roofing company needs good salesmen. I don't care where you go, you'll be able to make an above average income, probably well above average, in whatever market you end up in. That's freedom. That's peace of mind. That's the payoff."

By God, if that doesn't get their heart pumping, I need to stick a mirror under their nose to see if they're alive. That dream has become a reality for me and many of the people I've hired and trained. It's not pie in the sky. It's real, and it's obtainable.

By the way, Jeremiah Davies was the first member of the "A-Team" I hired at NVR in November of 2003. He was an ex-Marine and I loved him from the first minute I met him. He didn't get off to a great start. He really struggled, but he hung in there. More than once, he sat across from me all dejected and down in the mouth. I told him the truth. "Jeremiah, I have no doubt, none at all, not one little sliver, that you're going to succeed at this. Just hang in there." He did hang in there, and he succeeded.

The thing that caused Jeremiah to struggle in the beginning is the same thing that makes him so valuable today. He cared. He cared about his customers. He cared about making sure that what he was telling a customer was right. He cared about their roof and about the quality of the job. He studied and learned more than I will ever know about the different aspects of roofing and siding and skylights and many other things. He cared about the crews. He cared about his fellow salesmen and helped them every chance he got. And he cared about the company. He is the epitome of honesty and integrity and trustworthiness and hard work.

If I were going to start a new sales force today, it would delight me beyond words to have even one Jeremiah Davies on my team, regardless of the industry. (Ten like him would be a dream unworthy of contemplation.) I love that guy. He's still with NVR today, and doing very, very well.

The part that is so incredible for me to believe, even though I know it's true, is that Jeremiah is but one of the salesmen I hired that fit that description. Rob Livingston, another one fresh out of the Marines, is just like Jeremiah. He is a true professional … and he cares. He struggled out of the gate as well, but he hung in there. He studied and learned and asked questions. As he learned, his confidence grew and his closing ratios improved.

Ryan Doan was born to sell. He was quick out of the gate and learned from his mistakes. He too cares about his customers and his company. Joe Cotter struggled too, but he's still there … and making money. A few months ago, he closed his biggest deal to date, $300,000.00. He's just another example of what being a good person and trying to do the right thing can accomplish. They are all just down right good, honest, hard-working guys, professionals in every sense of the word. We are truly blessed to have them on our team.

One of the bad things about being in the consulting and restructuring business is that there always comes a time when you have to move on. For me, that time is nigh, with my next gig being a long term one, and over thirteen hundred miles away from NVR. I will miss those guys more than I can put into words. Deryl calls them my "babies", but she means that in the most flattering of ways, to them, and to me.

I have often heard that owners and managers shouldn't get emotionally attached to their employees. To that, I can only say, "Bullshit!" A good manager can scold and discipline and even fire a friend. I've had to do all three many, many times. Don't be afraid to get close to your people—at least not if you're the kind of person that they can learn to care about too.

I hope that you can tell that my love, respect, and admiration for them are genuine. And I sincerely hope that you can find, hire, train and keep a group of salesmen for whom you can develop these same feelings. If you can, then hit your knees every night and thank the god of your choice.

5

A Roofing Philosophy

Before you can train your new sales team, you must decide how you're going to install a roof. Everyone has different opinions on what is best. I believe that I've come up with a good roofing philosophy, so I'll share it with you. Obviously, I'm not going to explain every aspect of installing a new roof though. I will only mention those things on which I have an opinion that is contrary to the commonly accepted roofing practices (and some of them are contrary to what the "experts" say as well). Please keep in mind that I use many of these things to separate myself from the other roofing salesmen who will be giving the customer an estimate, and I teach my salesmen to do the same. That is my reason for mentioning them here.

Laying Over

Laying over an existing roof is easy, simple, and excuses the company and the crew of doing the nasty, dirty, time-consuming, expensive part of a roofing job. The problem is that the finished product is a piece of crap.

I have removed as many as seven layers of roofing from a home. Also, I've had many customers exclaim in frustration "I paid the last company to remove the existing shingles. I'm sure I did." I never have a good answer for them.

When laying over an existing roof, you can't inspect the decking for delamination, mold, or mildew. You can't install Ice and Water Shield. You can't flash the chimneys and skylights and pipe flashings and walls properly. In other words, you can't do a good roofing job.

I love to sell against companies whose salesmen have recommended laying over an existing roof, telling the customer "Code allows you to have o there's no reason for you to go to the extra expense to remove the existing shingles." Those are among the easiest sales I've ever made. It gives me a chance to demonstrate to the customer that I'm interested in doing a good job for them, even if it means doing the "dirty, nasty, labor-intensive, difficult" part of the job that the other companies aren't willing to do.

You can offer to do a half-assed job, or a thorough one. The choice is yours. I insist that any company I'm associated with refuse to layover, even if it means losing the job. You have to decide what's right and what's wrong, and then only do what is right, regardless of the consequences. Potential customers will respect that, and you will respect yourself for taking a stand. If that means losing a job here and there ... deal with it.

New Drip Edge

Always install new Drip Edge on the rakes. Wind-blown snow and rain can violate the shingles at the rake edges. Drip Edge won't prevent it totally, but it will send the snow or rain onto the top of the felt, if the felt has been installed under the Drip Edge as it should be. There is no way to get the new felt under the old Drip Edge, so you must install new Drip Edge.

If the rake board has "crown molding" on it, the Drip Edge may stick out some. Still, you should install it, but you'll need to warn your customer about this in advance. It is not usually a good idea to remove the crown molding though, as the Drip Edge will not extend down enough to cover the bare wood that was under the crown molding.

Also, many builders do not install Drip Edge when they build a new house. Some of them, if they are wrapping the fascia with aluminum, have their siding crew "lip" the aluminum out ½" or so at the top. I have no idea why they do it. It's worse than doing nothing. If you find this situation, your crew must deal with it somehow, because the new Drip Edge will most often not fit down over the "lip" properly. I've seen some crews cut off the "lip", while others chose to bend it down or up over the top of the rake board. Either way is a pain in the ass, but it must be done.

Gutter Apron

Standard Drip Edge should not be installed on the eaves. The eave flashing should extend down into the back of the gutters. There is no other way to prevent wind-blown rain or snow (or ice-damming) from getting behind the gutters, rotting the fascia board, and dripping down onto the customer's head or flowerbed. Also, there is often a gap in the fascia board behind the gutters. I've seen the gap as wide as two inches, but most often, it's about an inch wide. Without something to stop it, wind-blown rain or snow that goes behind the gutters can go right through the gap and into the house.

Standard Drip Edge does not extend down far enough (usually only 1" to one 1 ½") to lap into the gutters on the downspout end of the eave. Obviously, the gutters slope down toward the downspout for drainage. On long runs, they may drop two inches or more. Standard Drip Edge won't accomplish the mission in that situation.

I prefer to use a wider Drip Edge, and one that is a different shape. E-6" Drip Edge works nicely here. It is in the shape of an "L" with no lip. It extends 3" up under the shingles, and 3" down the fascia board and into the back of the gutters. If you are not changing the gutters, the E-6 must be "notched" to fit down over the existing gutter spikes. Again, it's a pain in the ass, but it should be done. If you are changing the gutters, have the roofing crew remove the old ones prior to installing the E-6. If you don't, the crew will notch the E-6. Then, when your gutter crew removes the old gutters, the notches (which are now unnecessary) will be there, allowing wind-blown rain, snow, and ice-damming to get to the fascia (and gap, if there is one). If the old gutters are removed, no notching is required to install the E-6. Then, the gutter crew can slip the back edge of the new gutters up behind the E-6, screwing the clips through the E-6 and the back of the gutters at the same time (making a much neater and more effective installation).

I explain why I use E-6 at the eaves to every customer (and I find a way to make my competition look like scoundrels for not using it).

Starter Shingles

Using special Starter Strips is a no-brainer. Back before the roofing industry got lazy, crews would use 3-tab shingles as starter, lapping the tabs into the gutter, and then cutting the tabs off (I have actually seen one crew do this since I've been in the business, but only one). This insured that the glue line on the starter course was down next to the edge and provided a good seal on the first main course. It worked great—no problem.

Somewhere along the way though, crews came up with a way to save some time. They began turning the 3-tab starter course backward. That way, they didn't have to waste all of that time cutting off the tabs. Obviously, the glue line is no longer down near the edge (it's 5–6" up from the edge), but they didn't see any problem with that. Doing it that way still provided a solid surface behind the first course so there would be a shingle covering the decking in the keyways of the first main course.

If covering the keyways is the only reason to install the starter course though, why do they use a starter course on architectural shingles that have no keyways? I don't get it!

Of course, protecting the keyways is not the only reason to use a starter course. We need to seal the bottom edge of the first main course to something to keep wind-driven rain and snow from getting under it. That's why those old crews went to all the trouble to cut the tabs off, so that the glue line would be down near the edge. Why give the wind, rain, and snow 5–6" of free access under the shingles?

Most shingle manufactures make special starter shingles, which are little more than 3-tab shingles with the tabs already cut off. They sometimes cost a touch more per bundle than a 3-tab, but when laid end to end, they cover more linear feet. So the cost of using special starter shingles is about the same ... sometimes even less than using 3-tab.

Now, let me get this straight: It's better, and it doesn't cost more. Hmm, surely every roofing company in America is using them. The truth is, very few roofing companies use special starter shingles. If you do (as I do on every job), and you find a way to explain it to the customer that makes you look like a hero for doing something "special" for them that the other companies don't do, and you explain to them why using 3-tab as starter (and simply flipping them backward) is bad, it might impress the customer. Personally, I use this as part of every sales presentation I make, and I teach my salesmen to do the same.

I also install special starter shingles up the rakes. The "experts" don't require it, and I've been told that it's not necessary, but I do it anyway. It makes sense to me. I think it makes for a better job, and I use that in my presentation as well. I do it … the other guys don't … so I'm better. At least that's how I present it to the customer. The additional cost is negligible.

Felt And Steep Roofs

Use heavier felt on steep roofs. I'm constantly amazed at how many roofing companies don't do this, and I'm just as amazed at how few roofing crews complain about it. It's a safety thing. On steep slopes, you can't walk flat-footed. You're either on your toes, or the side edge of your shoe. Either way, very little of your shoe is on the surface. As gravity tries to do its thing, thin felt can tear and you can fall off (or even worse, a member of the crew can).

I didn't know much about roofing my first year (I've already told you that.), but it only took me about two months to learn that simple lesson. My instructor for the lesson was a crew foreman named Marcus. He had two crews and they were both among the best I've ever seen. We were standing in front of a two-story house with a 10–12 pitch roof. I had ordered 15# felt for the job. Marcus put his hand on my shoulder, looked me in the eye, and asked me what the life of one of his crew members was worth to me. And then he explained the problem, "One of my men could die." and the solution, "Order 30# felt if the roof is over 7–12." I got it.

Since then, I have ordered heavier felt for steep roofs. I care about each and every member of my crews. Their lives are valuable to me … more valuable than the cost difference between using 15# and 30# felt.

Power Vents

The problem with Power Vents. Before I learned better, I recommended Power Vents on many jobs. My main selling point was "They don't vent your house in the winter when you don't need it anyway. Your heat won't all go through your roof and you'll save on your utility bill." Gawd! Was I an idiot or what? Well, I was new, and I didn't know any better. I thought I was telling them the truth. I know better now.

Virtually all of the "experts" agree (and that's really saying something) that the best ventilation system on a gable roof is the combination of soffit vents and ridge vents. However, steep hip roofs do not have enough ridge to use this combination, so they recommend installing Power Vents in that instance. I agree with them. (Isn't that a shocker?)

Regardless of the reason, there will be times when you need to leave a Power Vent where it is, or install a new one. Never, ever do either of those things without making sure that the Power Vent is connected to both a thermostat and a humidistat. A thermostat alone will not do the job. Don't you want to vent the attic in the winter? The house is warm inside and cold outside. When condensation forms, it can literally rain inside the attic. Look at the Coke or beer can that you just took out of the fridge. What does it look like after sitting in a warm room for five minutes? What does the table look like under it? That's why we use coasters, isn't it? It's insane not to vent the attic in the winter.

Never mix Power Vents with Ridge Vents. More is not better. When the Power Vent comes on, you don't want it sucking air in through the Ridge Vent, or any other kind of vent that is high on the roof. You want it draw air in from the soffit, just like a Ridge Vent does. Any kind of vent will draw air from its nearest available source. You want the intake to be low on the roof so that you get a good "bottom to top" air flow.

Some suppliers don't even stock Power Vents with a humidistat, or even a humidistat that you can purchase separately. Talk to your supplier and see if you can get them to stock some. If not, find out where you can purchase separate humidistats. Then, either supply them and have them installed on the Power Vent, or make certain that the customer knows to do that. If that's your decision though, make sure that you have the name and phone number of the supplier that sells them, the price, a recommendation on someone to install it, and his normal price for doing so. The more information you can give the customer, the more likely they are to actually do it. Saying "Gee, I don't know. You need to find one and have it installed though." just won't cut it.

Ice Shield

Where to install Ice and Water Shield. Of course, I believe (as the "experts" do) that I&W should be installed on the eaves, in the valleys, around the chimneys, skylights, and around other penetrations.

Along the adjoining walls? Hmm … well okay, even though I don't think it does much good unless there is no siding or bricks already installed on the wall. My problem with installing I&W along a wall that already has siding on it is that my crew can't slide the "sticky" material under the J-Channel and up the wall. Without doing that, you haven't protected the joint between the roof and the wall, and that's where the water is probably going to get into the house anyway. Unless the I&W protects the joint, how does it do any more good than properly installed felt?

Also, running the felt all the way to the wall and then putting the I&W over it doesn't make any sense at all. I know and understand why "the experts" recommend doing it that way, but I simply don't agree. They say that the roof and wall expand and contract independently from each other … and they do. If the I&W is stuck to both, it could wrinkle or tear. Okay, I'll buy that … but only if you don't attach the I&W to the roof in other ways, like staples, nails through the step flashing, and nails through the shingles. I don't understand how they can say that the I&W on the roof will "float" independently from that on the wall if it is secured in so many ways to the roof. I just don't get it. If I&W is installed over felt, the net result is "heavy felt". Ice and water can still go under it simply by going under the felt. You lose the benefit of it sticking to the decking.

The "experts" recommend that I&W be installed up the rakes, over the hips, and over the ridge. I would recommend that myself … if I was a manufacturer who wanted to sell more I&W. I don't see that the benefit (if any) is worth the additional cost.

Upgrades

The style of shingle that is best for the customer depends on his house. Don't sell your customer a high-end shingle on a 3–12 or 4–12 pitched roof just to increase the price of the job and your profit.

Low pitched roofs do not allow for enough visibility of the shingles to take advantage of the shingle's color, shading, design, or patterns that make it a more expensive shingle. Decide what shingle you would install if it was your house and then recommend that style of shingle to your customer.

The Best Shingle

The best shingle is the one that the salesman likes. I believe that all of the major shingle manufactures make a good shingle. I like some better than others, but that's a personal preference and it is not based on actual quality.

In a 3-Tab shingle, I like GAF simply because I've sold more of them and I know their colors better. It may sound silly, but that is the only reason I have for liking them. I believe that a salesman should have an opinion though, and he should not be hesitant to state it. Therefore, when a customer asks me about 3-Tab shingles, I usually say, "All of the major brands are about the same quality and price. I like GAF simply because I've used more of them and I'm more familiar with them. I'm not saying that they are any better than the others. If I were you, I'd pick the brand that has the color you like and not worry about the quality. They're all about the same." Then I show them the GAF sample and wait for them to pick a color. They usually do.

In an Architectural shingle, I like Elk. I just like the way they look. They have very distinct shading and more contrast than the other brands. I like that. Not everyone does. Some people like a more "toned down" or bland look. If so, GAF, Certainteed, Owens Corning, and Tamko are happy to oblige. I let the customer make that decision, but I'll have an Elk sample board in my hand and show them that one first … because *I* like the way they look.

There is another reason. Showing the customer an Elk sample gives me something to talk about that I can't talk about with the other brands. I've sold a ton of Elk roofs, and I've had problems on two of them, one in Virginia Beach and one in Wisconsin. (I usually have already told the customer that I'm from a "storm chasing" background and have roofed all over the U.S., if not, I mention it here). In both cases, the Elk rep was out at the customer's home quickly, saw the problem, acknowledged that something wasn't right with the shingles, and paid to have them replaced immediately … no fuss, no hassle, no ducking of responsibility. I like that and it usually impresses the customer. (It impressed the hell out of me, I can tell you that). I'm not saying that the other manufactures don't respond in the same manner, just that I haven't had those experiences with them (because I haven't sold as many of their shingles).

> Woodbridge, Virginia, 1999. I had already sold a new roof to a retired army general and we were in the process of picking a color and brand. He had a 30-year Certainteed, Weathered Wood shingle on his house (Certainteed has the lion's share of the Northern Virginia, D.C. area market). His roof was a 10–12 pitch with a nicely visible front view. I could just imagine how nice it would look with the distinctly contrasting Elk 30 year Weathered Wood shingle on it. He wasn't convinced. "I'm afraid to change." He told me.
>
> Please keep in mind that I was strictly a salesman at the time, working on commissions, and I'd already sold the job. I told him "I'll tell you what, if you let me put this Elk on your house and you don't like the end result, I'll pay out of my pocket to have it removed and another shingle installed." He was impressed with my commitment and he agreed. After the Elk roof was installed, he grinned from ear to ear while telling me how happy he was that I'd installed the Elk. I had gone out on a huge limb with him, considering that it was an $18,000.00 roof, but I was committed. You need to develop that kind of commitment, regardless of what brand you prefer and recommend.

Knowing Your Installers

The Experts forget who is installing the new roof. I love my crews and I respect them immensely, so forgive me for saying this, but the installers are most often uneducated, improperly trained, poorly supervised, and speak little or no English. That is the reality of who we have to work with. The best thing we can do is train them, and then check on them often enough to insure that they are doing it our way … most of the time. That is the world we live in. Our installers are good at what they do, but most of them are not free thinkers.

What would you say if I offered you $100 or even $150 a day to do what they do every day, ten to fifteen hours a day, five, six, or even seven days every week for the next several years … in ninety plus degree heat with seventy-five plus humidity … or in the frigid cold of Wisconsin in February? You would not take me up on it, and if you did, you probably wouldn't last a month. I love them. I respect the hell out of them. But I also understand who and what they are. You must do the same. And then you must develop a way of roofing that you can teach them, and on which you can depend on them to understand and comply with … most of the time. That's just the way it is.

> Falls Church, Virginia, 2003. One of the shingle manufacturer reps gave me a training video that showed their recommendation for how each stage of the roofing process should be done. In each section of the tape, they would show a schematic and explain how it should be done, and then they would show a roofing crew doing it. The problem was that in many of the scenes on the tape, the roofing crew was not doing things the way they were explained and for sure not the way the schematic showed. John Francis and I laughed until our sides hurt while watching it (mainly because the company doing the job was our main competitor, and the owner of that company was John's life-long best friend.) When we showed the manufacture's rep a few of the discrepancies in the tape, he was more than a little embarrassed.

The problem is that manufacturers care about selling the products they make. The only time they become concerned with the quality of the installation is when they are providing a warranty on it, or when defects ... installation cause their products to fail (which also causes them warranty issues). Suppliers care about moving product. They aren't affected at all by the quality of the installation. So who does care?

I believe that the National Roofing Contractors Association cares, or at least reason would dictate that they do. They provide the most comprehensive installation guidelines I've seen to date. Many of the manufacturer's quote them on installation techniques. I'm just not sure that all of their techniques are based on "real world" applications. In any case, I simply do not agree with some of their guidelines (even though I understand the reason for them).

If you are going to purchase a special warranty from a manufacturer, you must adhere to their instillation guidelines. That's one of the reasons why I don't sell those warranties. It would be virtually impossible to train your crews to do a roofing job "this" way sometimes and "that" way other times. I prefer to establish one method of installing a roof and then train my crews to install it that way, regardless of which brand of shingles is being used or what kind of warranty we offered the customer.

Different Strokes

Different Strokes: I have always been amazed at how roofing companies in different parts of the country roof differently. The suppliers stock the materials that their customers order, just like Wal-Mart stocks what their customers buy.

In Lafayette, Louisiana, the local suppliers had never heard of "step flashing" or "3–1 pipe flashings". I was stunned. Finally, I went to my tool box and got a piece of step flashing that I just happened to have, carried it inside, and showed it to the man at the counter of a roofing supply company. He examined it and then asked me "What's it used for?" They didn't stock pipe flashings because their customers all used lead pipe boots (which will last longer, but are down right ugly, in my opinion).

In Allentown, Pennsylvania, the supplier didn't stock Elk's spray paint. When I ask why (since he did stock Elk shingles), he said, "I've never had anyone ask for it." I got him to stock some, and he told me two months later that he couldn't keep it in stock "Our customers scarf it up faster than I can get it in." Duh!

In Alexandria, Virginia, not one of the suppliers stocked "bronze" turtle vents, power vents, or turbines. When I ask why, I was told "We don't have any call for them." I was flabbergasted, so I asked, "What color do the other companies install on a Weathered Wood roof?" And I was told "Brown". Gezzzzz. Brown is about as close to Weathered Wood as Silver is to Gold.

In New Jersey, I ordered "starter strips" and the supplier sent out old 3-tab that he wanted to get rid of. When I called him on it, he finally admitted that he didn't know manufacturers made special starter shingles. By the way ... he stocks them now.

Oh well, I'll try not to go off on a rant. I hope you get my point. Don't accept no for an answer on these things. Decide what materials you need to do the job right, and then demand that your suppliers stock them, even if it's just for you. In fact, it's great when they stock them just for you. I mention that to almost every customer "Sir, the reason I know that we're the only roofing company around who does all of these things is because the suppliers tell me that they have to stock these materials just for us, that none of the other companies buy them."

6

Train Them

Okay, we've set the stage. We've cleaned up our office and gotten it organized. We've developed a mindset about how our employees are going to treat each other. We've developed a roofing philosophy that we feel good about and will help us during our presentation. We've found and hired some new salesmen and put them in the right frame of mind to be excited about their choice to work for us. Now we're ready to train them.

Imagine yourself being in the office and unavailable to take calls, answer questions from the other office staff or salesmen, and unable to handle any problems which arise with customers, crews, or suppliers ... for three weeks. If you want to properly train a new group of salesmen, that's what you have to do.

I try to keep a group of new recruits in the classroom for three weeks before taking them with me on a presentation. That's a long time ... a very, very long time. So why do I do it? The answer is not a simple one. To understand it, you must first understand what I hope to accomplish during those three weeks.

It was just before three a.m. when I woke up in a cold sweat. I sat up in bed and tried to command my heart to return to beating at its normal rate.

My sudden movement woke Deryl, and she elbowed me. "Who was it this time, Sharon Stone, Kim Bassinger, or Demi Moore? Or was it all three at the same time?"

I was still too shaken to laugh. "No, it was Bill, one of my new recruits. It was his first day out on his own and he was calling me for some advice on an estimate he was giving."

She knew me well enough to know that I wasn't kidding. "That must have been some phone call."

"Yeah, it was," I said, still dazed. "You wouldn't believe me if I told you … it was incredible. He was on a customer's roof and he was describing it to me perfectly. He was worried about the transition area between the 9–12 pitch of the main roof and a low-sloped porch—and the condition of the mortar on the chimney. He didn't think it would hold the new counter flashing. He knew what he was looking at and how to describe it to me—and he recognized the potential problems. It was … incredible."

Deryl put her hand on my shoulder and said with a chuckle, "Wow! Sharon, Kim and Demi could never compete with that. Do you need a towel?"

If a new salesman drives out of the office parking lot for his first solo estimate knowing the basics of roofing, the terminologies to accurately describe to you what he's looking at, how to measure a simple roof, and how to give a basic presentation … you're one hell of a teacher.

But hopefully, that's not all you were able to accomplish during those three weeks. Think about it. You don't really know these guys. You spent an hour or so with them during their initial interview, and another hour hiring them later. And they don't know you either … or the company. You don't know if they were just putting their best foot forward during the interview, and they don't know if all of that "caring about the quality of the job and caring about the customers" was just a line of bullshit, or if you really meant it, and believe it … and live it.

The interview really starts on the first day of training. You have three weeks to get to know them, to find out if they are real people, good people, honest people, and hard working people. And they have three weeks to find out about you. Are you really what you made yourself out to be? Is the company what you made it out to be? Are you for real? You have three weeks to find out … and so do they.

Obviously, I can't go through every hour of three weeks of training with you, but I can give you a general idea of how I do it.

Set The Tone

I like to set the tone at some point during the first day of training. I usually wait until I catch them whispering among themselves or becoming distracted. This may sound cold, or arrogant, or harsh, or whatever, but I don't care.

First, I quote from (of all people) Danny DeVito, in the movie *War Of The Roses.* He was a very high-priced lawyer and was offering to give a client some free advice. He said: "I charge $500 an hour. When someone who charges $500 an hour offers to give you some time for free, I suggest you listen to him."

Then I look at my trainees and scold them. "I don't make $500 an hour, but I do make one hell of a lot, and I've put all of my other responsibilities on hold to spend this time with you … at no charge. In fact, I'm paying you to sit there and listen. So I suggest you shut up and pay attention."

I don't usually stop there though. I usually continue with something like, "If you really understood how valuable this training is, what learning this is going to do for you, how it's going to change your life … and your family's life, you'd sell your car, take out a second mortgage on your house, walk ten miles in driving snow to get here, and you'd give me all of your money just to teach you this stuff. That's why it irritates me so much when guys don't pay attention, or they are late to class. Not only is it disrespectful, it's a waste of my time … and my time is worth a lot. So far, you haven't been late, but this is the first day. I just wanted to give you a little preview of the reception you're going to get if you are. Any questions?"

If that turns them off, or puts them off, or creates any other negative feelings, I don't care. I'm trying to live up to one of the promises I made them during the interview and hiring process, to always let them know exactly where they stand with me. "You'll never have to guess about that. I'll come right out and tell you to your face." So far I've never had a trainee take offence. Or if they did, they got over it quickly.

Plan Ahead

Have a plan for each day of all three weeks before the first day of training starts. The worst thing you can do is stand in front of your new team on the first day (or any day thereafter) unprepared. Don't wait until the evening before to put together a plan for the next day and then have to scramble to get the training aids ready. You'll end up looking like an idiot.

Training Aids

Have and use a lot of training aids. I'm sure that you're an excellent speaker and a very interesting guy, but you can't expect people to sit there hour after hour and listen to you try to describe things to them. You should have a lot of drawings, pictures, and small materials ready and waiting. If you're going to be talking about Drip Edge, you should have already cut enough one-foot pieces to have one for each trainee, and one for yourself. That applies to virtually every material. Try to avoid having just one sample available and forcing them to pass it around.

Doll House

Have a demo house available, so you can point at various things as you talk about them. You can use your daughter's doll house, or build one. I had one of my people build a five-foot high, eight-foot long slope of a roof in the corner of our training room. It had a dormer, a valley, and a miniature skylight curb. It also had a rake board on one end, fascia board in the front, and gutters. It was very crude, but it served the purpose. It's worth doing.

The Bucket Theory

I started college late in life. My degree is in Psychology. The professors pumped me full of information until my head was about ready to explode. It was not the most exciting material, and most of them were not the most exciting speakers. I nodded off … a lot. Many times, I couldn't remember what we had covered only a few days before. But I could still remember all of the words to the song "Hot Rod Lincoln," which I had learned when I was a kid. While pondering that phenomenon and listening to a professor drone on and on about the difference between short-term and long-term memory, and about the effect of recall, I was able to visualize the concept in a way my brain could handle.

It matters less how many times you tell me something, than how many times I recall it on my own. Picture the journey from short-term memory to long-term memory as a series of buckets lined up in a row, each a little smaller than the one before it. Each bucket has a hole in the bottom. As the buckets get smaller, the size of the hole in the bottom gets smaller, relative to the size of the bucket.

The largest bucket is short-term memory. Everything you see, hear, feel, smell, or taste goes into that bucket. The hole in the bottom is large though, so it doesn't stay in there very long. It will flow out the bottom and be lost unless, sometime prior to it leaking out of the hole, you grab it and recall it. When you're finished dealing with it, that memory goes in the next smaller bucket. The hole in that one is smaller, so it will stay in there a little longer. However, it will eventually leak out through the hole and be lost unless, sometime before that happens, you grab it and recall it. Then it goes into the next smaller bucket. The last bucket is very small, but it has no hole in the bottom. That's why I can still recite the words to "Hot Rod Lincoln" and why I can still remember that the nomenclature of an army jeep is "an M-1, 51, A-1, quarter-ton, utility truck, 4x4, Sir!"

Most teachers do not understand that concept. They think that hearing something over and over is the key. It helps, but not as much as recalling it on your own. The teacher goes over some material and then later calls on one of the many students to recall it. The problem is that, for the remaining members of the class, it was repetition, not recall. They simply heard it for a second time. They didn't have to recall it on their own.

If you're training five guys and you take that approach, the other four simply hear the material for the second time. They don't have to recall it. What will most likely happen then, is that each will remember one-fifth of the material covered that day—the part that you asked them to recall—if they were indeed able to recall it. If they weren't able to, you probably jumped over to the guy who was waving his hand in the air and let him answer it. A lot of good that did.

Asking questions as you go is good; it keeps them involved … and it helps keep them awake. But it's not the best tool for teaching them in a way that will help them recall the information later.

Lunch

Breaking for lunch during the training day should be anything but a break. If you use that opportunity to head to your office and make some calls or catch up on some paperwork, you're making a huge mistake. I take my new guys to lunch almost every day. I pay, and that makes them a little more excited about going to lunch with me, even after having to sit and listen to me talk for the last several hours.

Lunch gives me the perfect opportunity to accomplish several things, not the least of which is getting to know them better—and them me. But that isn't my main reason for doing it. I will have already scouted out several neighborhoods that have a wide variety of roofs and I will detour through those neighborhoods on the way to the restaurant—not on the way back though. The first hour after eating is not a great learning time. Breakfast is the exception to that, if it was a light breakfast. I use the roofs in those neighborhoods to review the morning's lesson.

Have your digital camera with you, and when you run across something that they just don't seem to grasp, take a picture of it. Print the pictures out that night and give the guys a pop quiz the next morning—not a verbal one though. You want each trainee to recall it on his own.

Pop Quizzes

Have a lot of pop quizzes—written ones, not verbal. The only way to get every trainee to recall things on his own is to make them write the answers. The questions might be verbal, with you pointing to something on your demo house, but the answers must be written.

No Multiple Choice

Always make them recall the answers themselves. When he is on a customer's roof and describing something to you on the phone, you want him to be able to recall the terms or names for various parts of the roof or the materials on it. You don't want to have to ask, "Is it this, or is it that, or is it this other thing?" That is the result of a multiple-choice quiz. How many times have you said or heard someone else say, "I know this. I'm sure I do. I'll know the right answer when I see it or hear it." Sure you will, but you probably won't remember it a month later.

Many teachers think that saying, "I'm not going to give you the answer. I want you to go look it up." Is a great thing ... and it is—at least it's better than giving them the answer. But looking it up in the book is still repetition—not recall. Recall is still better. It improves long-term memory much better than repetition.

Tell Your Stories

It's one thing to tell your trainees, "Never go onto a roof on a windy day without tying off your ladder." It's another thing to tell them about the time (before you owned a cell phone) that your ladder blew over and you had to spend two hours up on a roof, finally having to hang from the gutters and drop to the ground. Or about your salesman whose ladder blew over, so he called the office. No one was available to help him, so the office girl called the fire department to go rescue him. Or about the guy whose ladder blew over, barely missing the customer and his four-year-old daughter, but did land on the customer's pride and joy—his fully restored '57 Chevy. They will remember things like that much better than, "Never go onto a roof on a windy day without tying off your ladder."

I like to end such a lecture with something that I've found very effective. "Now, sometime during your first ninety days out, one of you is going to forget to tie off your ladder. It's going to happen. I guarantee it. The only question is which one of you it's going to be."

Keep The Numbers Real

Many experienced roofing salesmen have told me how good they are at measuring. They will say something like, "I'm never off by more than a bundle or two. If the job is short more than that, your crew is throwing away shingles." My response is always the same, "Bullshit!"

I'm good. I'm probably better at measuring a roof than ninety percent of the salesmen out there, but I make mistakes. I read my tape wrong. I hit the wrong button on my calculator. I forget to measure a slope, or an over-hang, or a shed (especially if the customer is standing on the ground talking to me the whole time, or even worse ... is on the roof with me). I guess wrong on a "guessing roof" (roofs which twist and turn and change levels in the most imaginative ways a "genius" architect could dream up), of which there are many. I tell my trainees, "On those roofs, your tape measure is used simply to help you guess better."

> Virginia Beach, Virginia, 1997. I was on my way to show my supervisor, Bobby Powers, a difficult job on the Newport News side of the Chesapeake Bay Tunnel and get his opinion on it. A crew was starting one of my jobs on the Virginia Beach side of the tunnel that morning. (Anyone who knows that tunnel will understand that it can take an hour or three to get from one side to the other.) At eight a.m., my cell phone rang. It was the crew foreman. "Neal, I'm fifteen squares of shingles and felt short on this job."
>
> I responded harshly. "How the hell could you possibly know that? You can't even be finished tearing off the old roof yet."
>
> "Neal," he said firmly, "I've been doing this a long time. I don't need a tape measure to know the difference between a twenty square roof and a thirty-five square one."
>
> I turned around and headed to the job. I always keep my original sheet of calculations, so on the way, Bobby took out a calculator and began rechecking my numbers. "Here's the problem right here," he announced. "This times this doesn't equal this. You multiplied it wrong. There's a thirteen square difference."
>
> I had made a simple mistake in multiplication while doing my calculations. Had I looked at the roof with my eyes though, instead of just

my tape measure, I would have known that something was wrong, just like the crew foreman did.

Woodbridge, Virginia, 1999. I met an insurance adjustor on a roof. After agreeing to pay for a complete new roof, she began measuring and drawing her diagram. I was helping her stretch the tape and holding the rope that was around her on the steeper slopes. We were up there for over an hour. When we got to the ground, she looked at her diagram and sighed. "Neal, I have a problem. I can't make heads or tails out of my own drawing. I've never seen a roof this difficult to draw."

I chuckled and told her not to worry about it. "I'll come back out here tomorrow and measure it myself, do a drawing, and fax it to you with the measurements totaled." She thanked me ten times before getting in her car to leave.

As promised, I was on that roof the next day. I was up there for over an hour again. I did a drawing and put the measurements on it. When I got to the ground, I looked at my drawing and realized that I couldn't make heads or tails out of it. Finally, I sat down with my calculator and tried to add it all up. When I was finished, my total squares, including waste, came to fifty-six. I got out of my truck, looked at the house, and said to myself, "That's at least a seventy square roof."

When I got back to the office, I called the adjustor and told her that I was faxing over my drawing ... without totals on it. "I keep coming up with under sixty squares, but damnit, I know it's a seventy square roof. I just can't prove it on paper." She trusted me and told me to add enough waste to the job to get it up to seventy squares, so that's what I did. When the job was done, there were two squares of shingles left over. It was a lucky guess.

My point is this. You must teach your salesmen to use their eyes and judgment as well as their tape measure and calculator. The numbers they write down and add up can't be just numbers. They have to equate to what their eyes and common sense tell them.

To accomplish this, I have an exercise that I like them to get in the habit of doing on every estimate. On the pad where they are going to write down the measurements and do the drawing, I tell them to guess how big the roof is before they start measuring it. I want them to write their guess on the paper somewhere and circle it. Then, if the final total is substantially different than their guess, they should find out why ... even if that means measuring the roof again. This exercise accomplishes something very important. It gets them in the habit of using their eyes, as well as their tape measure. And, it helps them keep the numbers "real." If they do this on every job, and if they don't always assume that their guess is wrong and the measurements are right, they will catch many measuring/calculation mistakes before they give the estimate.

The Old Fashioned Way

Even though I'm going to give my trainees a very sophisticated computer program to generate their estimates (I'm just bragging ... I wrote it), I teach them how to do it manually during training. I want them to be able to calculate the size of the roof, fill out a complete Material Order, Labor Order, and Cost Analysis, by hand. That is the only way they will ever learn what goes into a roofing job, what it costs us, and what price they should charge the customer. I wait to introduce them to the estimate software until the last two or three days of training.

Some owners don't want their salesmen to know what the job costs. They are afraid that, if the salesman knows the profit margin, he might start getting greedy ideas or something. My response is always the same, "Bullshit!"

Part of training a new salesman is educating him about how expensive it is to run a roofing company. Once they know how much is spent on the office and equipment for it, office staff, insurance, utilities, advertising, legal fees, accounting fees, taxes, warranty issues, and the dozens of other things you have to pay, they will not have a problem with the gross profit margin. If, after you explain it, they aren't glad not to be the owner, then you didn't explain it very well.

Let's Go To The Movies

Spending the three weeks in the classroom to train three or more new salesmen is worth the time and effort. But what if you just hired one? Can you justify spending three weeks away from your other responsibilities to train one new salesman, and then take him out into the field and spend more time with him there. The answer is probably no. It would be nice if you could, but it's not realistic.

I was faced with this dilemma at NVR in early 2004. I had just spent four weeks training my second wave of new salesmen (three weeks in the classroom and one week in the field). Then, a few days later, I ran across a sharp young guy and decided that he was too promising to pass up. I made the mistake of thinking that I could simply have him sit in my office all day and I could train him between phone calls and other interruptions. It didn't work. Is it any wonder that he didn't last but a few months? I would like to be able to say that I learned my lesson from that, but I didn't. I tried it again with another sharp young guy later, and he failed as well—because I had failed him. I hadn't trained him properly or thoroughly.

> Stroudsburg, Pennsylvania, 2005. I was about to begin training the two salesmen I'd just hired for Stroudsburg Roofing. Seth Peyser, the owner, asked me, "Neal, how am I going to train new salesmen after you leave?" (I was only going to be there six months.) I thought about it and came up with an idea. "I'll video tape every hour of this training. Then, both you and the people you hire later can watch it." He liked that idea, so that's what I did.
>
> By the end of the first week though, it was obvious that it wouldn't work. When I'm in front of a group of trainees, there is always one or two who fail to grasp a particular point, or struggle with a concept. Their questions, and my repeating things over and over to get them to understand, resulted in a whole lot of tape made while teaching them a single lesson. We had hours and hours of tapes that one would have to search through to pull out a particular bit of information.
>
> Finally, I came up with another idea. I began conducting additional training classes on Saturday and Sunday (all day both days, from sunup to sometimes midnight, for several weeks) … but there were no students in the room. It was just me, the camera, the whiteboard, and the training aids. Everyone laughed later at how good I had done at pretending that there were trainees sitting in front of me. It was unique, to

say the least. When I was finished making the tapes, I transferred them to DVD and gave them to Seth.

Later, when I got back to Virginia, I told John Francis what I'd done. He loved the idea, so he asked me to make him a set of training DVDs that were geared toward his company. Now, when he hires someone new, he can simply give them the DVDs to watch and study. The advantage for the trainee is that he can watch a lesson over and over if he doesn't understand the material the first time through. And, he can use the DVDs for review later.

I'm not going to tell you that this is the preferred way to train a new salesman. It's not. It doesn't allow the kind of interaction and personal attention that a conventional training class offers. But it's better than no training, or bad training. It's better than having a new recruit sit around the office waiting for you to get a few minutes free to spend with him. And it's even better than doing what many of us have done, sending him out with another salesman. Don't do that—not if you want him to be trained properly. The best salesmen are usually terrible teachers.

Call In The Experts

It's good to let your new trainees hear from someone other than you. Manufacturer's Reps are usually happy to give you a hand, if you've scheduled well in advance. Actually, their mouths water at the opportunity to get in front of a group of new salesmen … and they pay for lunch.

I have learned from experience to set the ground rules going in. Many Reps will spend an entire hour, or two, or three, talking about their company, how big they are, how great they are, and all of that other crap. I don't like that. It's not what I invited them there to do. I let them know in advance that it's okay for them to spend a few minutes touting their company, but they have been invited there to help train my guys about "How a shingle is made and should be installed." Or about "How the baffle system on your ridge vent enhances ventilation." Or about "What criteria are required to qualify for your special warranty."

Often, Manufacturer's Reps will agree to take the new recruits on a field trip to their factory, if there is one within a reasonable distance. Usually, the Rep will pay for a van and driver, and the factory will have a nice welcome waiting for you and your guys … and food. These are great outings, but are usually better when done in the months after initial training, not during your three weeks.

Show Them The Money

If there is one thing that you're concerned about your trainees overlooking when they go out on their own, extra layers that must be removed, steep pitch, extra charges for mansard areas, and so on, challenge them not to overlook it … and sweeten the deal with some money.

Here's the way to do it, using the example of extra layers (a perennial favorite). Let them see you write a check for $250 dollars (or more, if you really want to sweeten the pot), but don't sign it, and leave the payee blank as well. Let them see you put it in an envelope and seal it. On the front, write: "Bonus for not overlooking extra layers." On the back, list their names. Then tell them, "The first time you overlook an extra layer, I'm going to scratch off your name. The last name left will be the one I make the check out to. I don't care how long it takes to get down to one name, a week, or a year, or five years, this check will be waiting for the winner." Then pin the envelope up in an obvious place (on the door of the sales office, or near their message trays, or some other prominent place) so that they will see it every day. This little exercise will probably save you many, many times the amount written on the check.

A lot of things in the estimate and sales process are habit for experienced salesmen. They do things without having to make a conscious effort to do them. You want new salesmen to develop good habits. The longer one is a candidate to receive the bonus (while making a conscious effort to check for the extra layers) the more the practice becomes ingrained into his routine.

> I was training a new salesman in the field. We were doing the final inspection on a job that had been completed the day before. As I was going up the ladder, I stopped to peek under the first course of shingles. My trainee asked me, "Neal, you know they removed the old

shingles. We were here yesterday and saw them doing it. Why are you checking for extra layers now?"

I shrugged and said, "Habit. I'm so used to checking for extra layers when I go up a ladder, I can't help myself. If I go up this ladder three or four times in the next ten minutes, I'll probably stop and check for extra layers every time. You need to develop the same habit."

Salesman, Inc.

Another conversation that I always have with trainees before kicking them out of the nest: "Guys, you need to start thinking of yourself as a business. You are Ryan, Inc. and Rob, Inc. and Jeremiah, Inc. and so on. You have an obligation to yourself and your family to do everything you can to make your business successful. You can't sit around on your hands and wait for us to do everything for you. You have to learn about new products, new technology, and stay up on the things that will make you more successful. And you have to put a percentage of your income back into your business. You have to spend money for clothes, equipment, and supplies, just like any business does. When you're in a neighborhood checking on your job, you can talk to the neighbors, and you can put out door hangers in the neighborhood with your business card on them. When you're at a service station or restaurant, go out of your way to prospect, talk to people, hand them your business card. Every time you have a few minutes when you're not running leads, or even when you're driving to and from an appointment, you should be thinking about new ways to help you grow your business and become successful. Do that, and you'll be way ahead of ninety-nine percent of the roofing salesmen in the world. And you'll become successful.

In early 2006, NVR bought a booth space at the Home Show in Reston, Virginia, on the far west side of the D.C. Metro area. John Francis asked Deryl and me to spend some time at the booth to help answer questions from the patrons. We had office staff there to set appointments, and salesmen there to interact with the public. On Saturday, by far the busiest day of the show, there were a lot of us there to help. I stood back and watched as the salesmen I'd hired and trained over two years earlier fielded questions and responded to them.

After a couple of hours, I went to the back of the booth and told Deryl, "I can't believe those guys. They know ten times more than I do. I've been standing there listening to them answer technical questions about things that I wouldn't have the first clue about. They had to have learned all of that on their own. I didn't teach them any of that stuff. God! I love those guys." I had to struggle to keep from getting all choked up.

Deryl just smiled. She knew what I was feeling.

Billboards

There is one more lecture that all of my trainees have to endure:

"I spent a couple of years in the billboard business. Billboards are subliminal advertising. They aren't intended to elicit an immediate response, except for those out on the highway that say "Holiday Inn, next exit" or something like that. A car dealership doesn't think you're going to see their billboard and develop an uncontrollable urge to drive straight to their dealership to buy a new car. The same holds true for realtor ads, liquor ads (hopefully), and ads for medical facilities. You see the ad, even if you don't read it or focus on it. You're eyes see it, your brain registers it, and if you see it enough times, you will become familiar with the business or product being advertised. It's all about name recognition.

"The same holds true for you. When you step out of this office, you are the company to everyone who sees or hears you. You've got our company name on your truck and on your shirt. It's important for you to give everyone who sees or hears you a favorable impression of our company."

"If you're in stop-and-go traffic, and someone is waiting to turn out from a side street, let them in. Don't cut people off in traffic or flip them off when they do something stupid. Hold the door open for people and smile and greet them in a friendly voice. Don't throw trash out of your window. Stop and help the man or woman push their stalled car out of the road."

"When that person gets ready to buy a new roof, they probably won't remember the name of your company, or even seeing you. But when they ʌellow Pages and flip through the ads, when they see ours, they ʌ get the warm fuzzies, and they won't even know why. When you show up at their door and they see the logo on your shirt, they will get those warm fuzzies again, but again, they won't know why. Most often, it will all be subconscious."

"In short, treat everyone around you like a potential customer. You are walking and driving billboards for this company. Make the ad a favorable one."

Training Outline

1. **Roof Types** (Gable, Hip, Mansard, Gambrel)

2. **Roof Parts** (Field, Rake, Ridge, Eve, Valleys, Hips & Soffit)

3. **Pitch**

   a. Why it's important to know it (Different Materials and Labor Cost etc …)

   b. How to determine it (Pitch Meters)

4. **Basic Shingles** (3-Tab, Architectural), and how they are made.

5. **Starter Shingles**

   a. Benefits of using them (instead of turning 3-Tab backward)

   b. Where we install them and why

6. **Ice Damming**

   a. What causes it

   b. What results from it (leaking, mold, mildew, rotten wood)

7. **Ice and Water Shield**

   a. Why use it

   b. Where we install it

8. **Other Materials**

    a. Hip & Ridge Caps, Felt, Drip Edge, Eve Flashing, Pipe Flashings

    b. Counter, Step, Apron & Pan Flashings

9. **Measurement Terms** (Square Foot, Square, Linear Foot, Actual, Go Back, & Waste)

10. **Coverages**

    a. 3-Tab and 30 Arch Shingles

    b. I&W Shield, Felt, Starter, and Hip & Ridge Caps

11. **Basic Measurements**

    a. Measuring a simple Gable roof

    b. Measuring a simple Hip roof

Notice that I made sure to go over the basic materials and coverages before getting into measuring. I do that because, after they have measured a roof, I want them to be able to calculate the Go Back or total squares of shingles that the crew will have to install, which is the number that we will charge the customer for. Obviously, if they don't know how many bundles of Ridge Caps and Starter they will need, they won't be able to arrive at that number. I don't allow them to simply add a percentage for those things, as many people do. I want them to be able to calculate it more accurately than that.

12. **More Measurements**

    a. Measuring Gable extensions

    b. Measuring Hip extensions

13. **Guessing Roofs** (Roofs that have no accurate way to measure them)

14. **Ventilation**

    a. Importance of proper ventilation

b.   Ventilation techniques

c.   Types of ventilation

15.   **Chimneys**

a.   Chimney Parts (Cap, Flue, Flue Cap, Head & Bed Joints)

b.   Chimney Flahings

c.   Crickets

16.   **Skylights**

17.   **Valleys**

a.   Closed Valleys

b.   Open Valleys

18.   **Low-Slope Roofs**

a.   EPDM

b.   TPO

c.   Modified

d.   Tying them in to pitched roofs

19.   **Exotic Shingles**

a.   Cedar Roofs

b.   Heavy Comp Shingles

c.   Slate

d.   Fake Slate

20.   **The Roofing Process** (from drive up to clean up)

21.   **Siding**

a.   Materials and Terminologies

32. **Role Playing and Practice Presentations**

33. **Watching me do presentations** (one trainee at a time with me)

34. **Me Watching them do presentations** (me with one trainee at a time)

Of course you understand that during each of these lessons, I'm filling in with all the little things that it would be impossible to list here. Things like safety, securing the ladder in the truck so it won't blow out, how to dress, body language, and many other technical aspects of roofing jobs and the roofing business (like how to handle difficult customers and such). But I hope this outline gives you a basic idea of the kind of flow and order I like to follow in my training classes.

How much time you should spend on each topic depends on how quickly your trainees grasp the concepts. You should insist that they have the measuring and basic materials and basic terminologies nailed before moving on. And then keep drilling them on those throughout the three weeks.

Also, if you are going to give them Estimate Software, you shouldn't let them run their first lead until you are sure they know the software backwards, forwards, and inside out. You don't want them bumbling and fumbling with it while sitting in a customer's driveway, or even worse, with the customer standing at the door of his truck looking over his shoulder.

7

Equip Them

Call a plumber out to your house to repair your toilet. He shows up with a set of plumbing tools. The same is true for an electrician, a carpenter, or virtually any other professional. It always amazes me to hear the owner of a roofing company say that a roofing salesman needs only a tape measure, a ladder, a calculator, a blank contract, and a pen to sell roofs.

True, some roofs can be sold using only those things. I used very little else during my first four years in sales, but that was in a storm chasing company and I was doing the job for someone else's money, the insurance company's, not the homeowner's.

Here is a list of equipment that I think a salesman should have. It's up to you what you supply and what he should supply for himself, but I believe that you should supply much of it. After all, the better equipped he is, the more money he will make you. After giving you the list, I will tell you which items I supply for my salesmen.

Please remember that I buy cheap, even when buying for myself. After all, many of these things will remain in my truck 24–7. I don't want to worry about them being stolen or damaged or lost. That's just a cost of doing business.

1. A ladder (28' minimum). I personally like to carry two, a 20' for easy access to shorter roofs, and a 32' for the really high ones. I am slender … and old, so I really struggle with the 32' ladder. It controls me more than I do it. That's why I recommend that most salesmen carry a 28 footer, for more control and less chance of an accident.

2. A ladder rack (if he has a pickup). I have used a Weekender (removable ladder rack) ever since I've been in the business, but there have been many times when I wished that I'd had a full ladder rack to carry multiple ladders or a box of siding, or a sheet of plywood on top.

3. A laptop. Yes, we want our salesmen to have a laptop in their vehicle. You'll understand why when we get into the presentation chapter. Buy a cheap one ($750 after rebate). The brand matters. We have used Dells, Compaqs, and Toshibas. Of those, The Toshiba brand laptops have seemed to take the extreme heat, the extreme cold, and the vibration of extended use in a vehicle the best. Remember, your salesmen are going to mistreat them. You can't judge how the laptop will perform and last by your experience with them in the home or office environment. I personally own three Toshiba laptops at the time of this writing. The one in my truck stays there 24–7, 365, regardless of the weather. It's 5 years old and has had no problems. The one I am writing this book on was the cheapest model I could find at the time. It's 3 years old and gets packed around a lot. My wife's is a wide screen Toshiba, two years old, and is packed around less. Of the 50 or so laptops I've purchased for various companies over the last three years (or dealt with after someone else purchased them), the Toshibas stand up to the abuse the best. That could be a fluke, but if you want a damaged laptop to repair, I have a pile of Dells and Compaqs lying around that I'd be happy to sell you … very cheap. (And no, Toshiba doesn't pay me for saying this, but they should. Perhaps I should contact them and see if they will.) One last thing: Warn your guys that if they connect the laptop into the internet, for any reason whatsoever, and get a virus, fixing or replacing the laptop is on them. I strictly forbid my salesmen to connect a company laptop to the Internet, but they do it anyway … and they have gotten viruses, and they've had to pay for new laptops. A word to the wise is sometimes wasted.

4. A laptop stand. This is a swivel stand that is installed in their vehicle without drilling holes. If you tell the supplier what kind of vehicle you have, they will send out the mounting brackets that slide under the

passenger seat bolts and an arm that swivels it out to within easy reach of the driver. It should not interfere with someone sitting in the front passenger seat. A note here: I have the kind that adjusts to the specific laptop, with adjustable clamps that can be positioned around the USB ports, power cord, and CD drive. I don't recommend that type, as it requires an hour or more to readjust it to receive a different laptop. Many of my salesmen have found the type that utilizes two rubber bands to hold the laptop onto the stand. I was skeptical, but they do work much better. You can change laptops without extensive, time-consuming adjustments.

5. A power inverter. I use one with two outlets that can be hard-wired to the battery instead of plugging into the cigarette lighter. I prefer that kind. I hard-wired mine myself in about an hour, and I'm about the least mechanically talented of any human you will ever meet. It should be at least 500 watts.

6. A printer. I personally prefer an HP that also scans and copies (aprox. $200), but most of my salesmen prefer the Lexmarks at closer to $60. I like the photo-print quality of the HPs, and I like to be able to copy and scan right there in my truck. I have used several different brands, but so far, the HPs have suit my needs better.

7. Extra print cartridges (black and color). Any salesman who goes out on an estimate without extra print cartridges is an idiot. In fact, my salesmen bitched so much about the cost of print cartridges, I started making extra cartridges the prize for winning weekly sales contest.

8. A digital camera. (You will understand this need more clearly when we get to the presentation chapter.) Go cheap (as long as they have a zoom). Your salesmen will drop them off of roofs. I prefer the ones that use 4 batteries, so I don't have to worry about the batteries running down too quickly. Don't worry about the resolution. The bottom-end ones are good enough. Expect to pay $200 for a decent digital camera.

9. Rechargeable camera batteries and a charger for them. The extra money spent for rechargeable batteries will be nothing compared to having to constantly buy new ones. I do, however, carry extra non-rechargeable batteries in my truck for emergencies. Also, warn your salesmen that viewing and printing pictures directly on the camera will exhaust the batteries very quickly. They should upload the pictures to their laptops to view and print them.

10. A file box. The plastic kind that has a handle, and no, the handle won't last a month. I have purchased many of them. I haven't found one yet on which the handle could withstand the weight of a box full of files and paperwork. The file box should also contain separators (A-Z) for filing estimates in alphabetical order. When a customer calls and wants to do business, you don't want to search through 200 estimates to find his. It should also contain some hanging folders to keep the various forms separate and easy to find. I recommend the full-size file box, about one foot square. It will stand up in the seat better, and withstand more urgent breaking than a half-size one. There are few things more irritating than having to pick up your paperwork from the floorboard, sort it, and put it back in the box, especially when you're pressed for time.

11. A pitch meter for determining the pitch of a roof and calculating the Up and Over from the ground. If you haven't taught your salesman how to use one properly, it's probably because you don't know how. GAF and IKO give them away for free. The other manufacturers probably do too, but that's just a guess. Of the two, I prefer the ones supplied by GAF. They are easier to use.

12. A 30-foot metal, retractable tape measure that will clip on your belt. If you are in a market with a lot of cedar roofs, you will also need an empty film canister with a slit cut in it to use with the metal tape measure. Simply cut a slit in the side of the plastic film canister, slip the lip of the tape into it, and bend it so it won't come out. The film canister will allow the end of the tape to slide over the cedar shingles without

catching on the edges or between the cracks. (Just one of the little tidbits you learn after measuring a few hundred roofs.)

13. A 100-foot cloth (not plastic) tape measure with a reel handle. There is a specific way to modify the design of the standard model found at most Home Depot or Lowe's stores. First, you have to cut off the clip on the end of the tape. It's difficult to do, but it can be accomplished with a set of wire cutters. Wrap the first 3 or 4 inches of the tape with electrical tape or duct tape to protect it from the sharp edges it will encounter. Otherwise it will fray and break (at the worst possible time). Next, work a small key ring (1") through the loop in the end of the tape where the clip was removed. Then, work a large barrel-style fishing swivel through the key ring. (At this point, you should have the tape attached to a key ring, attached to a swivel.) Next, buy a heavy, firm, rubber ball. I like the standard T-balls used in baseball T-ball leagues. (They look like a baseball and are the proper weight to prevent modest winds from floating them along the roof.) You can find them in quantity at Wal-Mart, Target, or Toys-R-Us (and many more places). Next, bend a heavy-gauge wire (just lighter gauge than a clothes hanger) in the shape of a U. Hook it through the swivel, and then force both ends of it deep into the ball, stopping when the middle of the U is as tight as possible to the ball and before the ends protrude out the other side.

You're going to all of this trouble for one reason, so that you can stand on the ridge of a steep roof, let out some line, and let the ball roll down into the gutter. After getting your measurement, you can simply reel it up. The swivel prevents the tape from twisting too much as you let it out and reel it in. When you're ready to measure the ridge, simply drape the ball over one end and stretch the tape to the other end. The ball will hold it in place if you don't let it get too much slack in the process. This all takes some practice, but believe me, it's many times easier and faster than measuring a large roof with a short metal tape that won't go or stay where you want it.

I also like to drill a hole in one corner of the handle part and thread a large (2"–3") key ring through it. I use the large ring to hang the tape measure on an open-ended hook on my belt when I'm not using it. (You can find those hooks in almost any hardware store.) I like to climb my ladder and go up onto a roof with my hands free.

There is only one drawback to using this setup. If you hang it from your side, and the customer has a dog, he will most likely take a shine to the ball, which is swinging along with every step you take. (Another of those little tidbits ... I obviously have a lot of them.)

14. A metal or aluminum tent stake. I prefer the aluminum ones with the hook on one end and a point on the other. They are used for measuring siding mostly, but can also be used when measuring a long eave from the ground. You simply stick the point of the tent stake through the key ring on the ball of your tape measure, and then stab it into the ground at one end of the eave or run that you want to measure. Then walk to the other end and stretch it tight. You don't have to worry about the ball rolling when you stretch it, or using multiple measurements with a short metal tape. It's easy and quick. You can substitute the tent stake with a live person to hold the other end of the tape measure for you, but I have found the tent stakes to be easier, quicker, and eat less.

15. A caulk gun. I use one for temporary repairs. Customers who have gross violations in their roofs, appreciate you making temporary repairs while you're up there measuring. You will "loan" your caulk gun to a crew sometimes, and you will never get it back, so be prepared to buy several of them every year. I prefer the cheap chrome ones that have a wire attached to stick down through the nozzle to penetrate the tube of caulk, roofing cement, or silicone. It should also have a cutter for clipping off the nozzle.

16. Several tubes of caulk, silicone and roofing cement. Note: I once heard Marty Haight say, "Caulk is a temporary solution to a permanent problem." I believe that is true. Never think that you have done your customer a good deed by sealing a leak with caulk, silicone, or roofing

cement. Use it to stop the leak until you can provide the customer with a permanent solution to his permanent problem.

17. Wire nuts, in a variety of sizes. If you believe as I do, that Power Vents should be used when there is no better option, then you will be having your crew remove a lot of them, and cover the holes with plywood. The crew will rip them out, without regard for the wiring left behind. You shouldn't let the wires dangle unprotected. Go into the attic and install wire caps on the exposed wires. And then tape the wire caps with electrical tape to keep them in place. Remember, the lives of the homeowner, his wife, and his kids may depend on that being done. Isn't that worth fifteen or twenty minutes out of your day?

18. A telescoping ladder. Who wants to carry a 20' or 28' ladder through someone's home to climb up through the door into the attic? I don't. I have done it many, many times. I have found a better way. I carry a telescoping ladder in the back floorboard of my truck. It's about 2 ½' tall and 18" wide, and it telescopes up to 12'. I carry it into the house in one hand without worry about knocking over an expensive vase. And it doesn't leave marks on a carpet or hardwood floor. It's especially useful when doing a commercial estimate and having to access a trap door from inside, or get over a locked cage on a roof access ladder from the outside. I love my telescoping ladder.

19. A pair of Cougar Paws. If you have not had the pleasure of walking on a steep pitched roof wearing a pair of Cougar Paws, you have been deprived … and you're tempting fate. Cougar Paws are designed and produced specifically for walking on steep pitched roofs with the most safety possible. They are high-top shoes with special soles that grab onto shingles or cedar and can be changed by the user in a few seconds when they wear out. Roofing professionals and insurance adjustors all over the world buy and wear them. They are incredible. I keep a pair in my toolbox, and I take the time to put them on before getting up onto any roof that is 7–12 pitch or steeper. Mine cost me $65 back in 1999 and I have gone through a half dozen sets of soles (pads) since

then. (The secret to the pads lasting is you taking the shoes off when you get down from the roof, instead of wearing them around all day.) The new "universal" pads work on both composition shingles and cedar. The shoes cost roughly $125 at the time of this writing, with the pads costing approximately $10 per set. What is your life worth? What is your salesman's life worth? I love my Cougar Paws. God bless the guy who invented them. (And no, the manufacturer of Cougar Paws doesn't pay me for saying so. I simply love them, and I firmly believe that every roofing professional should own a pair ... and use them.)

A word of caution: Never walk into a customer's house wearing Cougar Paws. The same pads that hold you on the roof, also collect gravel and other things that can scratch hardwood floors. And they soak up water, so they will destroy a carpet ... I've been there, done that.

20. Nice shirts with the company logo on them. Since people have different tastes in clothing, and because all types and styles do not look good on all people, I offer my guys a deal. "Go buy some shirts and bring me the receipt. I'll pay half, and then I'll get our logo put on them for you." They love that idea.

21. Signs for their trucks. If they live in a neighborhood that does not object to signs, I pay to have their trucks "lettered up" with nice looking vinyl signs (if the salesman doesn't object; if he does, I question his commitment). Otherwise, I buy them magnetic signs, but I hate those. I think they look cheap. They are better than nothing though.

22. GPS device and software. Since your salesmen are going to have laptops in their trucks, a GPS device is too good not to have. A good one, with software (covering the entire U.S.), costs only about $100. I'm addicted to mine.

23. A small clipboard. I like the small ones that I can tuck down inside my pants in the back. Like I said earlier, I like to have my hands free when I go up the ladder.

24. A solar powered calculator. I like ones with large numbers for easy reading when the sun is bright … but I'm old. I still have the same one that I bought at Wal-Mart my first day in the roofing business. It's helped me sell hundreds and hundreds of roofs. It's got some miles on it … but then again, so do I.

25. A cell phone. I hate phones with direct connect. I can't understand the other person half the time, and I sometimes get embarrassed when I can. I've tried to train everyone to ask right off "Are you clear?" but they keep forgetting. It's bad to be standing with a customer and some idiot comes on the thing and says, "Hey, faggot, get your kneepads on. I just signed a fifty grand deal." Or something many times worse than that. I finally got rid of the phone with the direct connect feature. I refuse to carry one again. You do, however, need to make sure the phone has a lot of minutes, or better yet, an unlimited plan. Your salesmen will be on it a lot, and so will you. Some carriers also have a GPS feature available, so you can log onto the web (or get your nine-year-old to do if for you) and see a map showing where the phone (and the salesman) is at a given time. Also, warn your guys that text messaging and e-mail and other such goodies cost extra and you'll expect them to pay for those.

26. A pair of cheap binoculars. Let's face it, sometimes a salesman just can't get up on a roof and he needs a better look at something up there.

27. A large bottle of Tylenol. That's not for him. It's for you. He should have it handy for you when you ride with him out to one of his jobs.

I'm sure that I have left some things off of the list, but those are the main things a salesman will need, other than paperwork and samples and nice presentation folders, and a lot of pens.

I supply my guys with:

1. Laptop

2. Printer

3. Digital camera

4. Cell Phone

5. Ladder

6. Shirts

7. Truck signs

8. Cougar Paws

9. 30' metal Tape Measure

10. 100' Tape Measure

11. Caulk Gun

12. Caulk, Silicon, and Roofing Cement (all in tubes)

13. Pitch Meter

14. File Box with A-Z dividers and hanging folders

If they can't afford the other items on the list, I will loan them the money up front to purchase them. I want them to be successful as quickly possible, and I want them to feel like a professional from the very first day out. Having the right equipment to do the job is a huge step toward that goal.

Do I lose my investment sometimes? Of course. That's just the nature of the business. Losing your investment in a new salesman is simply a cost of doing business. It's always a risk, but if you aren't willing to take that risk, don't hire new salesmen. Hiring them and then expecting them to succeed without the proper tools to do the job, is a formula for failure.

8

Software

I can just hear you now, "Oh no, not more computer stuff!" Yes, more computer stuff. It's time to let you in on one of the best-kept secrets in the roofing industry today: Roofing Estimate Software, and Roofing Office Software. There are a few of both on the market, but I treat them exactly like I treat the other roofing companies in the market I'm working in—I know they are there, but I don't pay any attention to them. I don't worry about what they are doing, and I don't worry and fret over how to compete with them; I just do my thing, with the full knowledge and confidence that mine is the best, and provides the customer with what is best for them. Therefore, in this chapter, I will describe those things that I know my software will do for you, and I'll ignore the fact that there are others that might be able to do the same or more. Selling my software is not the purpose of this book. Investigating that is your job ... if you're interested.

Roofing Estimate Software

Your new salesman is in the process of giving an estimate. Hopefully, he knows how to measure a roof and determine its pitch. He's checked for extra layers and the other things that will increase the cost of doing the job. The customer has already indicated that he doesn't know what kind of shingles he wants. He's looking for ideas. Damn! That means your new salesman has to work up multiple estimates for the guy. This could take awhile.

After measuring the roof and making his notes, he goes back to his truck. Instead of reaching for his calculator though, he opens the lid on his laptop. His roofing estimate software is already loaded. He's already entered the lead information with the customer's name, address and phone numbers, so he's ready to work up several estimates.

First, he enters the measurements into the software. As he does, he answers some fairly basic questions about each measurement, pitch, number of layers to remove, and so on. After answering some other basic questions, like ventilation modifications and such, he selects the bottom-end shingle that he's going to offer this customer, the middle-priced shingle he's going to offer him, and the high-end one he wants the customer to consider. Then he clicks "continue."

Magically, three Material and Labor Orders are generated, one for each kind of shingle. The software knew what kind of ridge caps to use for each one, what they cost, how many feet a bundle covers, what kind of nails to use for each one, how many square feet a box covers, how much they cost, and on, and on, and on. Your salesman is given the opportunity to make any changes he sees fit, and then the software generates a detailed cost analysis of the job for each shingle type selected. Lastly, it asks the salesman what GP% he needs to achieve to conform to your requirements. Once it has that information, the software tells him what price he must charge the customer for each type of shingle.

The customer just came out to his truck and asked him to do the estimates on all three types of shingles with and without the detached garage figured in. That means three more estimates, using different total measurements. No problem. The salesman simply tells the software to do three more, without the garage figured in. He didn't have to re-enter all of the measurements or other details on the job. He simply had to delete the garage measurement for the next set of measurements. Now he has six, in the time it would have taken him to do one.

But wait, he might want to give the customer another option or two. No problem. He simply tells the software to copy the measurements and other information over into an entirely new set of estimates, select different shingles, and voila! Now he has nine, or twelve, or more estimates … and he doesn't have to worry about the little things like some of them requiring wider starter, or special nails, or different step flashing. The software already knew all of those things about every kind of shingle in the database.

He needs something to give the customer though ... and he can't type worth a hoot. No problem. He's already got an unlimited supply of sentences and groups of sentences already in there and waiting to be clicked on. He can select them as a group, or one by one. If necessary, he can add a sentence, or ten, or change the wording on the fly. When he's ready, he simply prints them out. They already have the price on them, but he can change it if he wants.

By the way, did I mention that the software already knew how you prefer a roofing job to be done? It will already know where you want to install Ice and Water shield, and such things as "Do you want starter installed up the rakes, or just at the eaves?" It will know that, when you say you want to install ridge vent, you prefer this brand and style over that one, and on, and on, and on.

About the only thing the software can't do for your salesman is measure the roof and determine the pitch and how many layers must be removed ... but we're working on that, heh-heh-heh.

Of course, I've only scratched the surface of the benefits of using the software. It helps make a professional company and a professional salesman look even more professional. And it automatically generates the paperwork that will be turned in with the contract, so it helps the office too.

Purchase and use roofing estimate software, regardless of whether it's mine, or someone else's. Doing so will help your salesmen, your office, your business, and it will help you make more money.

◆   ◆   ◆

Roofing Office Software

The phone rings. The caller wants an estimate for a new roof. Your receptionist turns to her computer and, after typing in his name, address, phone numbers, and other information, she's ready to set him an appointment. That is a difficult thing to do in busy roofing offices with a number of salesmen. Rob likes to start running leads early, and then break in the middle of the day for his QC responsibilities and follow-ups with existing customers before running another new lead or two. Ken likes to start running new leads later, after doing his follow-ups and QC inspections. Joe has a wedding to attend tomorrow, and Al is out of town for a few days. To complicate matters, another office staff member is on the phone in the next room, setting an appointment with another customer. No problem. Your computer software knows all of that and displays a list of available appointment slots for the next several days, or more. Your receptionist simply clicks on one. The appointment is set and recorded instantly, making that slot unavailable for the other staff member.

You have an appointment in an hour with your Yellow Pages rep to talk about your advertising for the next year. Should you spend more or less on the ad next year? Is the ad working for you? You hit the intercom button and ask your accounting department how much you spent on the ad last year. Then you turn to your computer (or have an office staff member do it for you) and plug that number in. A report comes up showing you an analysis of your Yellow Page advertising for the past year: how many leads it generated, how many of them were actually sold, how much revenue those brought in, how much it cost you per lead, how much per sale and on and on. You may want a printout of how that compares to the performance of your other advertising sources. No problem.

James, one of your new salesmen, comes in and needs to borrow $500 to get his truck fixed. That's always a great time to review his performance and make suggestions. You turn to your computer and display an analysis on James: his closing ratio, his average GP%, the state of his Receivables, his gross sales, and how much he has coming in commissions on his next check. It's that easy.

A staff member in your accounting department opens the mail and begins entering material bills. There's one from ABC Supply on job number 3278 for $700. But as she enters it, she glances at the Estimated Material Cost on the job. That $700 put the total bills substantially over what was estimated. She investigates, finds the problem and corrects it, all made possible because she had that information available when entering the bill.

Maybe the supply company sent out a duplicate bill, or perhaps someone typed in the wrong job number, or perhaps the salesman underestimated the cost of doing the job. If it's the latter, she prints a detail on the job and puts it in your box so that you can talk to the salesman about it and find out where he made the mistake.

Your Production Manager is entering crew invoices, but they often make mistakes on them. Not all crews get paid the same for everything, and in a busy company there may be many crews. She doesn't have to remember that Jose Martinez gets paid $11 per sheet for decking (he's been working for you longer, or was simply a better negotiator when hired), while the other crews only get paid $10. The software knows what each crew gets paid for each item. She only has to click on Jose's name, and then click on the item (in this case decking), then enter the quantity.

I could list dozens of tasks like these which are difficult to accomplish in a busy roofing office, but which are made simple and easy with the right computer software. I hope I've mentioned enough of them to give you the idea.

Remember two things. First, a successful office is organized and coordinated. The right computer software can greatly enhance that. And second, the key to making good, sound business decisions is having information available on which to base those decisions. Perception is not always reality. In fact, it rarely is. You need solid, accurate information available to you. You need good Roofing Office Software.

◆　　　◆　　　◆

Here are a few of the screens you'll see, beginning with the Main Screen:

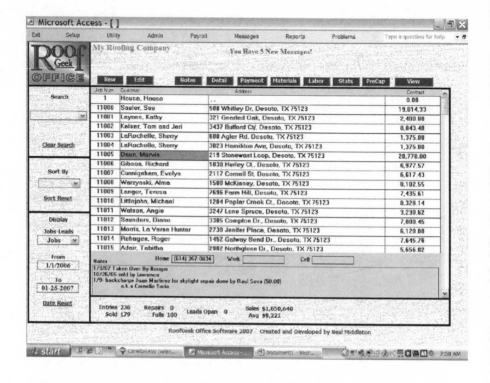

With one click of your mouse, you'll get this:

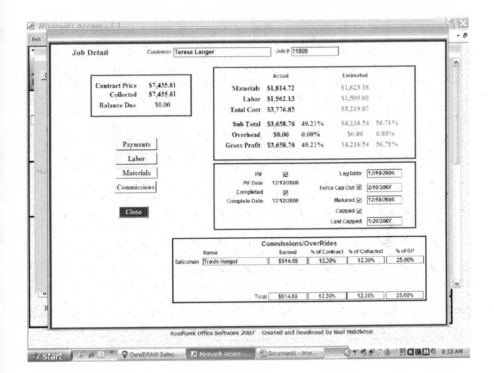

Or with one click, you can see this:

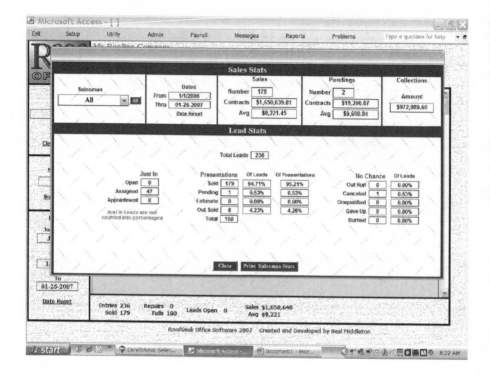

Or with two clicks you can see this:

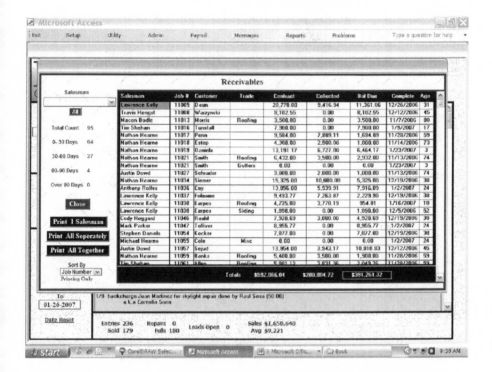

A different two clicks would get you this instead:

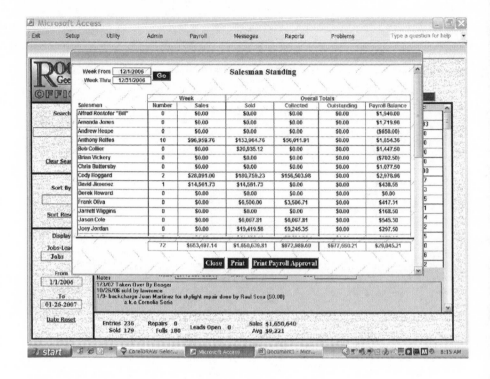

A different two clicks would get you this instead:

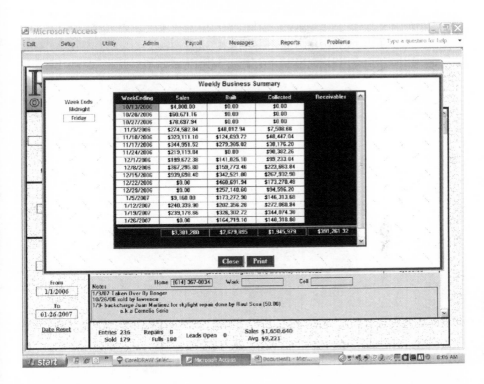

There are far too many such screens and reports to show you here, so suffice it to say that virtually any information you might need is no more than one or two clicks of your mouse away (surely even a total computer novice can handle that).

9

Those Valuable Leads

Advertising

The only way to get leads (other than by referrals) is by advertising. The old adage, "you have to spend money to make money," is right on. Most roofing companies advertise, but most of them don't do enough of it or do it properly.

Before you advertise though, you have to "brand" your company. You have to have a logo and a "look" that you will use everywhere. Logo recognition is no less important than name recognition. Make sure that your logo is clean, understandable, and easily distinguishable from other logos that the public sees on a regular basis. (Your last name may be McDonald, but I would shy away from using golden arches on your roofing company's logo.)

Regardless of where you advertise, you need to keep your ad clean, crisp, and uncluttered. Most advertisers make the mistake of trying to say too much in their ads. They want to utilize every inch of space. Big mistake! I fought this battle when I was in the billboard business, and later in the sign business. Almost every customer wanted to write a book on his billboard, or cram in another few logos of the products he sells.

You need to decide on three or four ideas that you want to impart to your audience, and display them in as clean, crisp, and uncluttered a way as possible. Those might include: "Family owned and operated"; "Residential & Commercial"; "Roofing-Siding-Gutters"; and perhaps a catch phrase that might hook the viewer, something like "The No Pressure, No Hassle, Peace of Mind, Company." (I just made that up, and it's terrible, but you get the point.)

If you don't remember anything else from this section on advertising, remember "clean, crisp, and uncluttered."

Next, you have to decide where to advertise. I suggest that you use the shotgun approach at first. Make a list of all the advertising sources available to you, and how much each costs. Decide how much you can afford to spend, and divide your money between as many of them as possible. Doing this is the only way to achieve an accurate comparison. If you advertise in X this month, Y next month, and Z the month after, you will learn nothing about which is the more effective and efficient advertising. The first month was still cold, the second month very rainy, and the third month was when everyone went on vacation. How can you compare the results of your advertising in that situation?

You need to control as many variables in the experiment as possible. Advertise in all three places over the same period of time, in the same area, using some way to distinguish which one of them generated a given call.

Remember though, advertising is as much subliminal as it is overt. There is a cumulative effect. One form of advertising will complement another, and both of them will do better over time. You can't judge any form of advertising after only one ad goes out.

Also, the Yellow Pages will almost always be the benefactor of other forms of advertising. The customer hears your ad on the radio, but he was driving and couldn't write down the number. When he gets home, he opens the Yellow Pages and finds your ad, calls you, and tells your receptionist when asked "How did you hear about us?" that he found you in the Yellow Pages. It was the radio that generated the interest, but it got no credit for doing so.

Don't be afraid to try new forms of advertising. John Francis wouldn't even consider advertising with Valpak. I finally talked him into it, and Valpak ended up being one of our most cost-effective forms of advertising. (I'll tell you how I talked him into it later, in the My Stories section of this book. It's a funny story.) The radio was the same way. I was skeptical, but John did it anyway. It worked very, very well.

Take a deep breath, swallow hard, and then commit to spending as much money on advertising as you can possibly afford. Mix it up, and scrutinize the results with more than your gut feel for how each form of advertising is doing. Make sure your staff knows to ask every caller how they heard about your company, and track the results ... track the results ... track the results. In case you didn't notice, it's important to track the results.

Referrals

Referrals are the easiest sales to close ... period. The purpose of advertising is to generate enough leads to allow your company and your salesmen to impress enough customers to build your referrals up to a point where they are a substantial part of your leads.

When you answer a warranty call, meet the customer, and work through his problem in a way that makes him happy, you're doing that for one reason (other than because it's the right thing to do)—you're doing it to generate referrals.

The roofing business is easy when everything goes right on a job, but when things go wrong, when you have a warranty call, you have a great opportunity to generate referrals. After successfully satisfying a customer's problem, a great line before departing is, "This is what it's all about, proving to you that you made the right decision when you picked us to do your job. I hope you won't forget it when one of your friends or relatives mentions needing a new roof."

Don't just sell before the job. Sell after it. Sell when the customer has a problem. That's the best form of advertising you can buy. Anyone can look good when everything goes right, but very few roofing companies capitalize on the opportunity to sell when things go wrong. I love the line, "When things go wrong, that's when we shine the brightest."

Lastly, when a referral comes in, your staff should go to any lengths necessary to determine which salesman sold the customer who made the referral. It's a pain in the ass, but it's worth doing. Most often, the caller will not remember to ask for a particular salesman, even though he should. Maybe he wasn't even told the salesman's name by the person who referred him. In any case, the minute they say, "I was referred by a friend of mine," the office staff member should ask as many questions as necessary to determine who made the referral and who the salesman was who sold the referring party.

By the end or your second year of using my overall business formula and philosophy, referrals should account for a large part of your leads. And that will drastically increase your overall closing ratio and profit margin.

Setting Appointments

Most roofing companies receive a call, write the information on a duplicate phone memo pad, and give a copy of it to a salesman. But which salesman? Is he too slammed with other things to call that customer today? Will he call them tomorrow, or the next day? Did the potential customer call from work or from home? If your salesman does call, will he be able to catch the potential customer, or will he have to leave a message? If he leaves a message, will the customer return his call? Will the customer be too busy to talk right then? (He wasn't when he called your office, but that doesn't mean his isn't now.) How many times will your salesman call before he gives up? How stale with that lead get before it gets run ... if it ever gets run? Will your salesman pre-qualify him on the phone and decide that it's not worth making the hour drive out to the customer's house?

Leads cost money ... a lot of money. Depending on the advertising that generated them, a lead can cost $50, or $100, or even $150 to generate. Of course you won't know that unless you have a way to track and analyze your advertising, but let's assume that you do know it. Let's also assume for this discussion (just to keep things simple) that your overall cost per lead is $100. I've seen it a lot higher, and rarely much lower. In fact, it's not unusual for the lead cost per sale to be $400 to $700 (a fact that stuns most owners when they see the actual numbers).

How would you feel about handing a salesman a $100 bill and then watching out of your window as he lit it on fire, dropped it on the ground and walked off, without even taking the time to watch it burn? I thought so. That's exactly what happens every time you hand him a lead that he doesn't eventually run, for whatever reason.

We can put an end to that. It's not that difficult. All we have to do is set the appointment with the customer while we have him on the phone. By doing so, we solve all of the problems mentioned at the start of this chapter, and we stop the salesman from "burning" the lead. Or at least we make it a lot easier to find out if he does. We'll know that if the customer calls in to complain that no one showed up for the appointment.

Potential customers who have called two or three other roofing companies for estimates are pleasantly surprised when our receptionist says, "Okay, let me get some information from you and then we'll get you lined up with an appointment." They didn't hear that from the other companies, and they are impressed. (That's not a bad way to start with them, huh?) There are simply too many benefits not to do it.

First Out vs. Last Out

Man, talk about some heated discussions! This one always gets me off to a bad start with an experienced sales team (that I didn't train). Most salesmen believe that it's better to be the last estimator out. Most car dealers think so too. You can hear it in their ads: "Shop around and then come see us." In fact, almost everyone believes that being the last out gives the salesman a better chance of making the sale.

When I arrived at NVR, I fought that battle for months. John started in the business as a salesman … a very good salesman. He wanted to be the last estimator out, so he had trained his salesmen to believe and do the same.

During one sales meeting, one of our manufacturer reps was in attendance. After another heated debate with the salesmen, I asked John for his opinion. "Last out … always. I won't do it any other way." Courtroom attorneys have a saying, "Never ask a question that you don't already know the answer to." Obviously, I screwed that one up. I didn't learn quickly though. I turned to the manufacturer's rep and asked for his opinion. "I prefer to be the last one out," he said, further adding to my misery.

TJ, the most experienced of the salesmen in the room (other than John and me) spoke up. "Neal, you've never sold roofs here. You're a storm chaser. It's different in that situation. Storm sales are easy, but this is a very competitive market. Your way just won't work here." Of course, I was not surprised to hear him say that storm sales are easy. Most people think that, at least most people who haven't tried it.

I made another mistake. I got mad. "Oh really, then why don't you try it. Move to a new town in a new state, and open an office. You won't be listed in the Yellow Pages. The BBB never heard of you. You'll have out-of-state plates on your truck, probably no signs for your truck yet, and maybe even no business cards printed yet. For sure, you won't have any references, because you haven't done a job there yet. The local TV news and newspapers are warning homeowners to be suspicious of people coming in from out of town to work. Everyone can tell by your accent that you're not from around there. You don't have any leads to run because you haven't done any advertising. Now go out and knock on a few doors and see how many of those 'easy sales' you can make." That shut TJ up … and everyone else in the room, including John.

They all knew that I had sold more replacement roofs than everyone else in the room combined. Hearing the circumstances under which I'd done it, gave them pause, at least enough to accept a proposal. I would run some leads, test my theory in their market, and then report back to them on the results.

Of course, at that time, I had been basing my opinion of "first out—last out" on a theory, a hypothesis, not on experience. But (as with a lot of things), I was convinced that I was right, and I was committed to it. My theory was simple. To sell roofs in a non-storm situation, one should:

1. Commit to a method of roofing that is better than what the other companies are doing.

2. Design a sales presentation that is the most professional in the market—high on education, low on pressure, and with an impressive package to leave behind, including color photographs of problem areas on the customer's roof, and a typed, line by line explanation of what you're going to do on their home.

3. Most importantly, be the first out, so that you can set the standard for how all who follow will be judged. Educate the homeowner about things that you want him to ask the next guy, knowing full well that the next guy won't have good answers.

4. Don't try to close the deal on the first trip to the customer's house.

Prior to my heading out on the first lead, John told me that he would be elated if I could close 25%. His guys weren't doing that well. I closed 33%, and that number grew to over 45% after I'd stopped running leads and more of my customers called in wanting to do business. John couldn't believe it.

A few days later, we had another meeting. John spoke first. "Guys, Neal's way works. I'm going to turn the meeting over to him so that he can explain how you're going to sell roofs from now on." Obviously, he was impressed with my performance in the field over the last thirty days ... or at least with the results.

I would like to be able to tell you that John is a total believer now. He's not. His method of selling was very deeply ingrained during his years in the field. But John is no fool either. The first out method is working for his sales force ... and it's working very, very well. So, he bites his lip when the subject comes up. That is all I can ask of him.

Pre-Qualifying Leads

Unfortunately, this is another one of those battles I have to fight everywhere I go. No one likes to waste an hour driving across town, only to find that the customer is an unreasonable, arrogant, jerk who can't understand why, while the roof is being done, you can't build him a new dormer or pour him a concrete porch. Or, he's going to be selling his house in two months, so he's not the least bit concerned with quality. He just wants it to pass the home inspection so he can sell it. I understand that all too well. The problem is, if you pre-qualify leads, you will be missing out on a lot of very nice jobs.

Ken was on call for emergency repairs. His phone number was added to the recording on the office voice mail. It rained that weekend, and he got a call from a man in DC with a leak. After talking with the man, he decided that it didn't sound very promising, so Ken called Joe and asked him to handle it. Joe agreed, went on the lead, and sold the man a new $300,000.00 roofing job. (True story. It happened in 2005 in Virginia.) Joe was elated. Ken was pissed. You just never know.

One more example. I tell every new salesman the story of Joe Porto, the customer that I will never, ever forget. It was spring of 1998, Appleton, Wisconsin. It was early in the storm and I was running a few telemarketing leads. I hated doing that. Most of them were garbage. When I got to the Porto home, Joe wasn't there, but his wife was. She was the typical sweet little old lady. I inspected her roof and found that it had severe hail damage. She wouldn't sign a contract though. "You'll have to wait and talk to Joe. Would you like to come in for some pie?"

Three hours later, my cell phone rang and I got my first exposure to Joe Porto. His voice was rough and hateful and nasty. "This is Joe Porto. What the hell were you doing up on my roof?" I took a deep breath and tried to explain that his wife had invited us out, and that he had severe hail damage. "Oh yeah! And just how much of that damage did you do yourself while no one was looking?"

I'd never heard such venom. It was terrible. Finally, in a tone that I hoped would match his, I said, "Just call your insurance company. They'll take a look at it, and then you can call me back and apologize." And I hung up without waiting for him to respond. I knew I'd heard the last from him.

Two weeks later, my cell phone rang. "This is Joe Porto." His voice and tone were no different than the first time he'd called me. I gritted my teeth and asked him what he wanted. "I'll be home all afternoon. Get over here and bring whatever you need me to sign." And he hung up abruptly.

I couldn't believe it. But I wasn't about to pass up a job, so I drove over to his house. He was no different in person than he was on the phone. He was gruff and nasty and sarcastic, but he signed the contract. Then he took me to his neighbor, and then to his sister, and on and on and on. By the time I left Wisconsin for the winter, Joe Porto had been responsible, directly and indirectly, for me selling over fifty jobs. During subsequent visits to his home, Joe would give my wife a sack of freshly picked tomatoes and other items from his garden, and then he would turn to me and say in that same hateful, gruff, nasty voice, "Come back next week and I'll have some more." That was just how he talked to everyone, including his wife and friends.

Now, how many of us would have bothered to drive to Joe Porto's house the first time, if we'd talked to him on the phone first? I know I wouldn't have. Don't let your salesmen pre-qualify leads. They should run every one. If you have more leads than they can run, hire more salesmen.

Lead Distribution

Which lead do you give to which salesman? The answer is simple, but accomplishing it is not. The answer is: Give the next lead to the next salesman in line. There are three exceptions though. Of course, referrals are given to the salesman who sold the referring party. Secondly, if it's a "special" type of lead, and you have a new salesman who hasn't been trained on that special product or service, give it to him … and go with him and train him on it. The only other exception to this rule should be when you have your sales team divided into categories like Residential, Commercial, and so on. If that's the case, make sure that you don't have a Residential Salesman competing against a Commercial Salesman in sales contests and so on. In the perfect world, every salesman would be qualified to run any type of lead … and that should be your goal.

If you want to see the morale of your sales force destroyed before you even get it rolling, just let them find out that you are "cherry-picking" the good leads for yourself, or for your "favorite" among them. I've heard all of the arguments for "matching the lead to the salesman" and "increasing the likelihood of a sale, and the company's profits, by matching the lead to the salesman's skill, knowledge, or talent." But it will poison the morale of your salesmen.

A lead came in for a full replacement of a large, expensive, slate roof. John just happened to be in the office, so the receptionist asked him who she should give the lead to. "Give it to one of the new guys and I'll go with him on it to train him." Which of course was the perfect answer.

John spent a lot of time with Eric on that estimate and trained him well. They got the $135,000 job. So what happened when the next slate lead came in? John said, "Give it to Eric. He'll know what to do with it." That, of course, was the worst possible answer (okay, second worst; he could have taken it himself). But if every slate lead is now given to Eric "because he'll know what to do with it," how are the other four new salesmen going to learn about slate and learn what to do with it? Obviously, they never will, and Eric will win Salesman Of The Month … every month, because he is given all of the big slate leads. Try explaining that to the other four new salesmen. The correct answer would have been, "Give it to one of the new guys, other than Eric, and I'll go out with him and train him up on slate."

Remember, those leads don't mean just closing ratios or Salesman of the Month to your salesmen. They represent the chance to make money, to succeed, to pay their bills, and to provide for their families. If they have to watch another salesman make all the money, buy a beautiful new truck, win all of the sales contests and so on, just because he's being "spoon fed" the best leads, they will resent it. Their morale will suffer, and they will begin to question whether your company is the right one to work for. Every salesman wants an equal chance to succeed, and you owe him that. If one of them isn't worthy of running a certain type of lead, fire him and replace him with someone who is.

And don't think you can keep it a secret either. You can't, not over the long haul. Hopefully, you didn't hire idiots, so don't fall into the trap of thinking that they won't know who's getting what kinds of leads … and everything else that goes on in the office.

Salesmen Should Sell

Don't make the mistake of promoting your salesmen into management positions too quickly. It's tempting, but remember the Peter Principle, which states that "every person will be promoted to their highest level of incompetence."

The military is the best example of that. A good soldier is promoted to squad leader. He's okay at filling that role, a good follower, a great example for the other men in his squad, and they like him enough to do what he says, but he's not great at it … he's just good enough to get by without getting into trouble. Eventually though, the company needs a new platoon sergeant. He has seniority over the other squad leaders, so he's recommended for promotion. Now though, the job is all about scheduling and organization and paperwork. He's no good at that. He's not bad enough to get demoted, but he's not good enough to get promoted out of that job. He's stuck right where he is … at his highest level of incompetence, at the highest job that he's not bad enough to get fired from. That system is great, don't you think? I don't.

Don't promote your best salesman to sales manager unless he has demonstrated the skills required for that position. Being a great salesman isn't the prerequisite for being a great sales manager. Being a great manager who understands the sales process is.

Regardless, no person can be a great sales manager over the long haul unless he is out there selling roofs on a regular basis. He has to be able to say, "I'm out there doing the same thing you're doing every day, and here's what I'm running into."

Most sales organizations promote their best salesmen out of sales. Duh! "We've got three of the best salesmen in the world, but they just aren't selling right now." What sense does that make?

Marty told me during the first month that I owned my own company, with him as my silent partner and supplying the credit for our business, "Neal, remember that you're the best salesman you have. Don't stop selling."

Just in case you haven't picked up on it yet, I believe that Marty is one of the most business savvy people I've ever met, regardless of the type of business. His company will do over 100 million in re-roofing gross sales this year. He's worth listening to … on virtually any topic. (Except blackjack. The first time I ever met Marty, we got in an argument over blackjack odds. I'm right, he's wrong … I don't care how smart of a businessman he is.)

No Wimps Allowed

You've spent hours admonishing your salesmen to treat every lead like gold. You've set lofty goals for them regarding closing ratios, and you've let them know that you'll be monitoring the results. But there are two other things you need to teach them about leads. First, the customer is not always right, and second, they don't have to tolerate being disrespected by anyone, not you, not your office staff, not other salesmen, and for sure, not a homeowner.

Appleton, Wisconsin, 1998. Marty asked me to take a new salesman out with me on a few estimates to show him how I do things. I didn't like doing that, but I agreed, as a favor to Marty. I did, however, insist that we run the new guy's leads, not mine. By that time, I had become proficient at generating my own leads—very high quality ones that I closed 14 out of 15 of with consistency—so I wasn't taking any leads from the office.

The second lead we ran together was a call-in to the office from a flyer that had been sent out. It was almost an hour drive to the customer's home out in the country, but we managed to show up ten minutes early for the appointment. No one answered the door, but we heard a lawn mower running out back. There was no fence, so we walked around the house. The homeowner was on his riding mower, with his can of beer sitting on the hood. It was a very hot day, and he looked miserable. When he saw us, he turned off his mower and waited for us to make our way across the large backyard.

I smiled and introduced us. "I'm Neal, from Best Construction, and this is my associate, Tom."

"Well, it's about f ... ing time," he spat at us hatefully.

I kept my cool. "Excuse me, our appointment is for three, and we're ten minutes early."

He wasn't impressed. "Yeah, yeah, you're here now, but how about the other fifty f ... ing times I called. All of you f ... ing roofing people are too f ... ing lazy to drive out here."

I stared at him for a second and then slapped Tom on the arm. "C'mon, we're out of here. We don't have to take this shit." And Tom and I headed for the truck. The homeowner was right behind us, trying to apologize, practically begging us to look at his roof, but we didn't even slow down. When we were in my truck with the motor running and ready to leave, he was still at my window, begging me to look at his roof so that he would have something to give to his insurance company.

Finally, and without turning off my motor, I reached into my file box and got out a blank contract, put it on my clipboard, and handed it to the homeowner. "Sign that, and I'll consider looking at your roof. If your insurance company pays you for a new one, the job will be mine. Otherwise, we're out of here."

After staring at me for several seconds, he grinned and signed the contract. Tom and I got out, inspected and measured his roof, then filled in the blanks on the contract, gave the homeowner a copy and drove away.

When the insurance check arrived, the homeowner called me to come out with some samples. That surprised me. I didn't think I'd ever hear from him again, contract or not. When I arrived at his house, he was waiting on the front porch. To my further surprise, he apologized again for his behavior during our first meeting.

"I was on vacation, very hot, and very drunk," he told me. "I'm not usually like that." Later he said, "Neal, the reason I didn't even consider letting anyone else do my roof was because I hate wimpy salesmen, in any business. You weren't willing to take shit from me or kiss my ass, not even to get a nice deal like this one. I respect that."

You need to make sure that your salesmen know that they don't have to put up with that kind of crap just to sell a roof. Besides, it always makes me feel good to reject a customer. I'm usually laughing and slapping the steering wheel as I drive off after telling a homeowner, "Mr. Smith, I don't need your job bad enough to let you talk to me that way, so I suggest you find yourself another roofing company." It feels good to be the one dishing out the rejection sometimes.

Dispositions

If you are going to require that your salesmen provide you with feedback on the outcome of the leads you give them, you have to have a system for using that information. The last thing you want is to listen to, or read, a long explanation about what happened on every lead. You don't have time for that, and neither does anyone else in your office.

The feedback that you get on leads must be formatted and organized in such a way as to provide you with actionable intelligence—information that you can use to evaluate your advertising, the proficiency of your salesmen, your price, and your presentation. I have narrowed the possible "dispositions" or "status" or "outcomes" on leads to the following:

1. **Open.** The lead has not been assigned to (or given to) a salesman and no appointment has been set with the customer. (Only used in companies that do not set the appointment during the initial phone call.)

2. **Assigned.** The lead has been given to a salesman. (Only used in companies that do not set the appointment during the initial phone call.)

3. **Appointment.** Obviously, an appointment has been set with the customer, but the lead has not been run yet (or at least we haven't been provided feedback on the outcome yet).

4. **Canceled.** The customer called in and canceled the lead or appointment before we got out there, regardless of the reason.

5. **Estimate.** The salesman has run the lead and given the customer an estimate (written or verbal).

6. **Disqualified.** The customer wanted work done that we didn't want to do, or there was something else about the nature of the work that caused us not to want to get involved in it. Salesmen will often abuse this disposition, using it for all kinds of things. You must make them understand that it has a very narrow definition.

7. **Outrun.** Another company got the job before we got to him. I'm not sure why salesmen are hesitant to admit to getting outrun on a lead (unless they are setting their own appointments and are letting the leads get stale). Outrun simply means that another company got their first and sold the job. Our salesman never had a chance to give a presentation or an estimate.

8. **Outsold.** We gave the customer an estimate, but another company got the job. Okay, I can understand why a salesman is hesitant to admit to this … but he shouldn't be. If I am selling four out of ten presentations, then I'm getting outsold on six out of ten of them, and that's not bad in a tough market. In fact, it's very good. Your salesman shouldn't be hesitant to say they were outsold, even though it sounds bad.

9. **Sold.** Yeah! Congratulations! We got the job.

10. **Burned.** This is a bad one, but it's going to happen. I burn a lead on occasion. I don't intend to, and I try to avoid doing it (obviously), but it happens. That's life in the real world. Sometimes I am handed a lead that I just never get around to running. Perhaps the office even set me an appointment with the customer, but I had to cancel the appointment because something came up … and I never managed to get back with the customer. That is a burned lead. It's bad, but it happens to all salesmen. They need to be honest about it.

Brutal honesty is the key to turning these dispositions into actionable intelligence. You are going to be making many serious decisions based on the feedback you get from your salesmen. You may drastically change your advertising portfolio, sometimes by thousands, or even tens of thousands of dollars. You may tweak your sales presentation, or spend thousands of dollars on better sales materials. Your salesmen must be made to understand the importance of being brutally honest when providing the office with feedback about the outcomes of leads.

There is only one way to know if your salesmen are being brutally honest when providing feedback on leads: Check on them. Call homeowners yourself, or have another office staff member do it. Otherwise you may find yourself at the end of the year staring at reports, and trying to make serious decisions, all based on numbers that you don't have confidence in.

I had a Company Commander in the army that had a sign on his door that read: "The men only do right what they know the boss will check." I know that sounds a little pessimistic, but it's truer than we would like to admit. I believe that it was President Ronald Regan, when dealing with the Russians, who coined the phrase "trust but verify." He was an effective leader of people … and a very smart man.

Lastly, to get your salesmen to provide you with quality feedback, you must have a way for them to do it. If they have to sort through hundreds of names and try to remember what happened on those leads, the information won't be accurate and they will complain about doing it until you finally relent. A good computer software program will make this easy and simple. Make sure that the office software you choose has a way to print out feedback reports on leads that your salesmen can scan down and update quickly and easily.

All of the dispositions or outcomes listed above are final dispositions (meaning that they will not change later, or the likelihood of them changing is so remote it is not worth considering), except for two. Active (non-final) dispositions include Appointment and Estimate (add Assigned also if you are not setting the appointments for your salesmen). They are active because their disposition can change. Leads with active dispositions are the only ones which should show up on the salesman's feedback report. He shouldn't have to sort through all of the others to update the active ones.

10

Presentation Psychology

We've already laid the groundwork for the presentation. We have designed our roofing philosophy with the presentation in mind, adopting methods we can talk about to the customer while explaining how we're better than our competition.

Also, we've organized our office, inside and out. We've built a place of business which conforms to high standards of professionalism. The salesman in the field can feel good about our company and have confidence that he isn't pulling the wool over the customer's eyes when he talks to them about our level of commitment to quality and professionalism.

We've purchased and installed computer software that will assist us in tracking the progress of a job, from the initial call through paying the salesman and crew and all other bills associated with the job.

And we've trained and equipped our salesmen to represent us in the best possible way. After all, the customers won't buy us. They don't know us, apart from what our salesman tells them and perhaps their personal research on the Internet or through checking with consumer organizations. They buy the salesman, not the company.

But there are a few more topics we need to cover before we can talk about the presentation itself.

Preparation

The sales presentation should start before the salesman leaves the office, or his home. Does he have the paperwork he'll need, the samples, fully charged camera batteries, extra printer cartridges, samples, and the other tools and equipment he might need?

Has he entered the customer's lead information into his estimate software so that he won't have to fumble with that while sitting in the customer's driveway? Has he plotted his course to the customer's address, in his GPS, or on his map?

Arrival

A few months after I returned to Virginia from a long-term consulting job in Pennsylvania, John Francis asked me to attend a training meeting. The local manufacturer's rep was going to be sharing some things with his sales force, and John wanted me to listen in. I was no longer in a supervisory position with the NVR.

Not long into the meeting, the topic of arrival time at a customer's home came up. The manufacturer's rep strongly advised that salesmen do their best to arrive exactly at the scheduled appointment time. I had personally hired and trained most of the salesmen in the room, so it wasn't a surprise when most of their heads jerked around toward me to catch my reaction.

Had I still been in a position of authority with the company, I would have reacted more strongly, but I tempered my response. "If they do that, they're ten minutes late." I said in a polite and rather subdued tone. The rep shook his head and replied, "We don't agree. We don't think it's a good thing to show up before the customer is expecting you. He might be in the middle of something."

Had I still been in a position of authority with the company, I would have stood up and shouted, "Bullshit!" Then I would have probably asked him how many residential re-roofs the "genius" who came up with that stupid idea had sold in the last five years. I probably would have followed that with a dissertation on anxiety, and how varying levels of it affect both parties involved, how the various electrical emissions of the brain begin flip-flopping, how the galvanic skin response shoots off the scale, how the heart rate speeds up, how the blood pressure elevates, and how drastically you have diminished your chances of making a positive initial impression if you show up exactly on time, or worse, one minute late. I would have explained how a customer's anxiety level rises with each second of uncertainty about whether the salesman is going to show. After all, he may have postponed or even canceled other plans to be there to meet the salesman. Then I would ask him, "Hmm, are my watch and the customer's perfectly synchronized?"

But most of the salesmen in the room knew how I felt on the subject and why. When I tell a group of trainees in class, "Always show up at least ten minutes early. If you show up right on time, you're ten minutes late." I don't stop there. I explain why. So, most of the salesmen in the room didn't need a reminder. It's not often that I take a pass on butting heads with the "experts" on some of my stronger held beliefs, but I did this time.

I often show up at a customer's home as much as thirty minutes early. Of course, when they come to the door, I apologize for being so early and ask them if it's a problem for them. "If you're in the middle of something, I have plenty of paperwork to do in the truck." Most often, they are delighted that I showed up early.

Anxiety

As you will soon see, I will mention anxiety several times when talking about the presentation … and for a very good reason. Everything we do in life, from the second we're born, to the instant of our death, and every second in between, is for one purpose and one purpose only: anxiety avoidance/reduction. Anxiety is not just a mental thing; it's also a physical one. When we experience anxiety, our body undergoes changes that make us uncomfortable. Hunger creates anxiety, so infants cry to get relief from it. The lack of money creates anxiety, as does loneliness, being too cold or too warm, or being afraid of something. A phobia is simply a state of anxiety taken to an extreme. Each and every breath we take is to relieve or avoid the anxiety caused by the cells in our brain and body being deprived of oxygen.

If our visit to a customer's home lessens his anxiety level (beginning with his initial call to the office and having the appointment set immediately), and the visit by another company's salesman raises it, that customer is more likely to invite us back to his home, even though he may not even understand why or even be consciously aware of it. Much of it will happen in his subconscious.

Anyone who has ever invited an insurance salesman, or encyclopedia salesman, or burial plan salesman, or time-share salesman into his home knows what I'm talking about. The salesman never comes in empty handed. He usually has a flip chart, that most dreaded of all hand-held manipulators. And we all know what comes at the end of a flip chart presentation … the first attempt at closing the deal. But we stand our ground. "I need to think it over. I'll give you a call in a couple of days." You can almost see the salesman's brain doing cartwheels. He's been trained, drilled over and over, and practiced for hours for this very moment … the moment when we state an objection. He's a master at overcoming them. He knew what we were going to say before we did, and he knew what his response would be, how we would react to his response, what our next objection would be, and how to overcome that. Like I said, he's been trained to do it, and he's good at his job.

How high was your anxiety level when you let him in the door? How quickly did it elevate? And how high was it by the time the salesman finally turned the contract toward you and held out his pen? If you do finally manage to get that guy out of your home without signing anything (especially a check), how likely are you to call him up two or three days later and invite him back? My guess is "not very," even if you really would like to own a nice set of encyclopedias for your kids.

Even if you're a slow learner, after two or three of those experiences, you will begin to recognize the visual and verbal clues that you're about to be set up for another one. We've all heard about Pavlov's dogs. He would ring a bell and then feed them. After awhile, he only needed to ring the bell to make their saliva glands begin flowing anxiously. The bell was the stimulus, and the salivating was the conditioned response. For many of us, a flip chart is the stimulus and the conditioned response is our anxiety shooting off the scale: shortness of breath, increased heart rate, tightness in the pit of our stomach, and pure dread. How could we let ourselves get sucked into this again? We clench our fist, hoping that as long as it is clenched the salesman can't slip a pen into it.

For some homeowners the stimulus may be something as simple as the salesman asking to come inside, or the sight of a flip chart, or a clipboard, or even the pen stuck in his shirt pocket, threatening to jump out and into their hand. For others the stimulus is more verbal. We recognize the "pre-objection handling," things like, "If I can get the cost of this down to a manageable range, is there any reason why we can't do business today?" Or it might be, "Are you looking to make a decision and move on this thing right away?" Or any of the other slick little phrases some smooth talking, slick dancing master of the hard close uses. Whew! It rockets my anxiety level into outer space just thinking about it.

As I go through my presentation with you later, you'll notice many things that I say, don't say, do, and don't do, simply to lower or avoid raising the customer's anxiety level. I want them to have a pleasant experience with me, and a comfortable one … even if much of it is in their subconscious mind.

One-Legged Presentations

Much is made in most sales training classes about having both parties present for the presentation. This is simply to remove the "I'll talk it over with my husband" objection. I'm sure that I've lost deals because I gave my presentation to one spouse and another salesman presented to the other, and the one I presented to lost the battle between them. So what? I simply don't worry about it. I trust the numbers … period. I know that, in any given market, I'm going to make X number of presentations and close at least X number of sales as a result.

We live in a time when it's very difficult to get even one spouse home in the middle of the day, and almost impossible to get both of them there. I don't want to limit my schedule to working only in the evening, especially in the winter when it gets dark early. (I love daylight savings time for just that reason.) Also, evening is the time for the customer to have supper and spend quality time with spouse and kids, not do business.

Often, even when both the husband and the wife are home, only one of them will come outside to talk to me. I don't like going in the house. Inside is their territory, their comfort zone. The front yard is mine. I'll talk more about that later.

I usually feel more comfortable talking with the husband, simply because I assume that he will understand more of what I'm saying, with less explanation. However, I have given hundreds, if not thousands, of presentations to women. I am very often surprised how many of them understand the more technical aspects of what I am trying to educate them about. Also, women are usually more intuitive and are more likely to base their buying decision on their feel and trust and comfort level with me. Since I consider those to be my strong points, I don't mind that at all. I like to think that I'm good at instilling trust and confidence, so I don't mind the buying decision being based on those. In fact, I prefer it. Of course, I try to elicit the same emotions from the husband, hoping that those will add value to the more technical aspects of the job that I cover during the presentation.

The bottom line is this: Sell the one in front of you, and don't worry about it too much.

The Big Company

For some reason, many salesmen like to brag about the size of their company. I've heard dozens of salesmen exaggerate the size of their company to proportions that are ridiculous. I don't do that. In fact, regardless of the size of the company I'm selling for, I usually tell the customer (if the subject comes up), "We're a medium-size company, large enough that you don't have to worry about us going out of business tomorrow, and small enough to give you personal service and not let you fall through the cracks." That line works well and usually garners a smile or nod from the customer.

The Canned Pitch

I don't use one. I hate them, and I suggest that you don't use one either. Using a canned sales pitch is wrought with problems. Distractions, interruptions, oddities with the particular job, and many other pitfalls await the user of a canned sales pitch.

I simply talk to the customer about his roof and what we're going to do to it. I have a list of things that I'd like to slip into the conversation though. Sometimes I get them all in, and sometimes I don't. Often the customer is rushed, having not allotted enough time for a full estimate and presentation. I don't like that, but I deal with it. I simply give them an abbreviated version and try to hit the things on my list that I think will have the most impact on their buying decision. The more of the items on my list I'm able to slip in, and the more detail I'm able to go into on each one, the greater my chances are of making the sale.

When the customer is pressed for time, remember the importance of his anxiety level. If he is late for something and you are making him later, his mind is on that (and how to get rid of you). He won't remember the details of what you tell him, and he won't remember you fondly. You will be associated with high stress and high anxiety, even if it's only in his subconscious.

Body Language and Tone

I firmly believe that your body language and tone are as important as what you say. With practice, you can use them to add emphasis to a particular point, or to disarm the customer who has done his research and thinks he knows everything about roofing.

I try to maintain a very level, nonchalant tone, especially when talking about my company or myself. I don't want to appear to be bragging about either. In fact, I usually joke those things off. I also try to be nonchalant about most of the standard details of the job, the ones that most all companies do the same. I save direct eye contact and a more firm tone when talking about something that we do differently. I want those to have an impact on him. I want him to remember them. The rest of the time, I'm usually walking back and forth in the front yard, staring at the roof, and pointing to things while I talk. That changes when I get the customer to the tailgate of my truck to show him the various materials like Drip Edge, E-6, starter shingles and so on.

I make a conscious effort (especially when dealing with women) to keep my body language non-threatening. I don't stand in front of them much. I prefer to be standing to one side with both of us looking in the same direction. That's usually not difficult, since we're out in the yard and I can pretend to be looking at something on their roof. If I am facing them, I keep a distance that I sense is comfortable for them.

The best combination of tone and body language is confident and authoritative without being pushy or arrogant, and always non-threatening.

A Piece Of Cake

I've watched many salesmen treat a customer's concern like a piece of cake … and actually use those words. The customer will mention a concern, or ask about a problem area on their roof, and the salesman will slough off their concern by saying, "No problem. That's a piece of cake." That salesman just passed up a wonderful opportunity to make a good impression, to set himself and his company apart. If dealing with that issue is a piece of cake, then any company can do it right. The better response would have been, "Yes, that is a concern. I've run into that situation a lot of times, and it's never easy. We'll have to pay special attention to that area to get it right, but we're pretty good at it." Hopefully, you understand what I just did. I acknowledged that his concern was valid, and let him know that I would give it special attention. Otherwise, he will probably be out there during the job, staring at that area to make sure that it is dealt with properly. I don't want him doing that, because he doesn't know what "properly" is. Letting him know that I'm concerned about it will usually relieve his anxiety about it, because he will trust me to see that it's done right.

The Other Guys

You should never directly degrade another roofing company. In fact, even when you're telling the customer that you're going to do something the right way, or the best way, and that the other companies don't, you should excuse them. "That's the way it's been done for years. That's the way they learned to do it. We did it the same way until we discovered that wasn't the best way to do it."

Even when telling the customer, "They have to do it that way to keep their cost down on the job," you can add, "That's really the consumer's fault, not the roofing company's. Many homeowners just look at the price, not the quality, so roofing companies have to cut corners to keep prices down in order to get the jobs. We don't do that. We'd rather lose the job than cut corners to get it. After all, we're the ones who are on the hook for the warranty, so we have a vested interest in doing the job right."

I just told the customer that the other guys don't have our level of integrity or dedication to doing a quality job … without saying it in those words. I turned it into a positive for us, and a negative for the other guys, without blatantly slamming the other guys. I also gave the other guys an excuse: "It's the consumer's fault." And earlier: "That's the way it's been done for years."

I did something else too. I just told the customer that consumers are idiots for just looking at the price, and I implied that he shouldn't be like them. He should care about the quality, not just the price.

But that's not all. By saying, "We're the ones who are on the hook for the warranty …" I planted the seed in the customer's mind that we actually honor our warranties, otherwise we wouldn't care about that. I didn't come right out and say, "The other guys don't honor their warranties, so they don't care about the quality of the job." But that was the implication.

When I really want to say, "The other roofing companies are idiots and scoundrels for not doing it this way," I usually opt for, "I don't know why all companies don't do it this way. It may cost a little more, but it's worth it. And since we started doing it this way, we've had fewer warranty issues to go back out and correct." Again, I accomplished the goal, managed to slip in that we actually honor our warranties, and implied that doing it any other way will result in problems later.

When you come right out and talk bad about others, it makes you look bad … so don't do it. Find ways to take your jabs without telegraphing the punch.

Negotiating

In most markets, especially in the larger ones, there are people from many different nationalities and cultures. In many of those cultures, negotiating is a way of life, it's expected, and if you refuse to do it, you are insulting the other party. The Washington, D.C. metro area is the best example of that, with virtually every nationality and culture represented in great numbers.

It may sound cold or devious to say so, but the fact is that when dealing with a customer from a "negotiating culture," you must allow room in your estimate for that. But there is a catch. Your estimate will probably already be among the highest the customer gets, if not the highest. If you tack on some for the purpose of negotiating, you run the risk of increasing the "sticker shock" to a level where you will never get the opportunity to negotiate it back down. I handle this by adding a little to the price, and then letting the customer know with a wink, "There might be a little room in there to play, but not too much." If you just arbitrarily drop the price without a fuss though, then it will be obvious that you had it padded from the start, and the negotiating will continue.

Ross Perot explained better than anyone I've heard, how important it is to understand the person you're dealing with. He gave this example:

> Two American businessmen were driving through the desert in an Arabian country. They came upon a tent that had a camel tied to one side. For whatever reason, the two Americans decided that they wanted the camel, so they stopped their car and got out.
>
> When the Arab resident emerged from the tent, one of the Americans asked him if he would consider selling the camel. The man didn't react quite the way they expected. "Are you crazy? That camel has been

in our family for years. It's a pet. My children grew up riding that camel. It would destroy their young hearts to part with the camel. I could never sell it, and I am insulted that you would even ask."

The two American's quickly apologized and hurried back to their car. They were driving away when the Arab's wife came out. "What was all of that about?" Her husband shrugged and said, "Two Americans wanted to buy that broken down old camel, but they ran away just as I was starting to negotiate."

On a more personal note, my wife and I were vacationing in the Dominican Republic, courtesy of ABC Supply on one of their annual trips to reward their best customers. While I was catching some sun (and enjoying the views on the tops-optional beach), my wife walked down the beach to a group of tents where the locals were peddling souvenirs.

She found something she wanted to buy, asked the price, paid for the item, and began walking back to me. The man whom she'd just bought the item from chased her down. He was obviously an honest man and his conscience had started to bother him. When he caught her, he asked her why she had paid his asking price. "Why didn't you negotiate? I would have taken less." My wife explained that she was not good at that kind of thing. The man told her, "In our country, you must always negotiate." And then he reached in his pocket, handed her some of her money back, and sprinted back toward his tent.

You must learn to understand and respect people from other cultures, and deal with them in ways that make them respect you and show that you respect them.

Hunger

Just as an animal can sense fear, customers can sense hunger. If you really, really need to close one particular deal, you probably won't. If you've had a bad month and you don't have enough money to pay your bills and you're getting desperate so you start pressing a little harder, your closing ratio will go down, not up.

Regardless of your financial situation, you have to force yourself into a mindset that there is no one deal that is any more important than any other one … and none of them will make or break you. You have to trust the numbers. You have to believe that you're going to close X number of deals out of X number of presentations, and then go out there and deliver each presentation in a relaxed, nonchalant, "it's no big deal," routine manner. The better you can pull that off, the more of those presentations you will close.

No one wants to eat in an empty restaurant. There must be something wrong with the food. No one wants to buy from a desperate salesman in an old, broken down, poorly maintained, noisy truck. He must not be any good, or what he's selling must not be any good, or there is something else wrong with him or his product if he's that desperate. In real estate, the old saying is, "Sell in a Cadillac, and buy in an old Junker," or something to that effect. It makes sense.

If you haven't made it yet, if you're still struggling, you must learn to "fake it till you make it." You must appear unconcerned about the prospect of closing the deal. You can accomplish that with a little "self talk" on the drive over to the customer's house. When I was still struggling, I got into the proper mindset by constantly telling myself: "You only close 3 out of 10, and this next one isn't going to be one of those 3. Neal, just suck it up and go on over there and go through the motions on this one so you can get it over with, and then you can get on to one of the 3 that you're going to close."

Self talk takes practice. It can be either productive or destructive. Make sure that yours is productive.

Humor

If I can't get a customer to laugh at least once during my presentation, I know things are going poorly. I try to show the customer that I don't mind laughing at myself, at my company, at my competition, or at him.

11

My Presentation

Obviously, it will be impossible to go through my entire presentation word for word. I do it differently every time, and every situation is unique. I can, however, give you a good idea of how I do it.

The Initial Meeting

I arrive early, knock on the door and introduce myself. I already have my business card out and ready to offer. Then I ask (as I'm backing down the steps, hoping that they will follow me), "So, have you already got an idea what you want to do on your roof, or are you looking for ideas?" This is no more than a fishing expedition. I want to know if they've been researching, or if they've already had other roofing companies out to talk to them. While I'm waiting for them to join me in the yard, I'm staring up at their roof and deciding what kind of shingles I'd want on it if it were my home.

I walk around the house, looking up at the roof, hopefully with the customer close behind me. I point to various things on his roof and talk about them with him, things like algae, or a valley that runs into a wall and will need special attention. I even talk about things on the ground. If he's got a new deck or special tile on the patio or something that may need special attention to protect, I'll point it out and say, "Don't let me forget to mention that on the contract if I end up with your job. I'll need to make sure I point it out to the crew. I try to get out here a couple of times during the job to make sure it's going the way I want it to, but sometimes they beat me out here. I'll have to remember to put that on the work order and talk to the crew about it just in case." I just scored big points with that. I let him know that I'm concerned about his property and that I'm not going to disappear after the contract is signed, that I'm going to see his job through to conclusion.

Step In To My Office

Of course, my truck is my office. After getting a good idea what the prospective customers want, I usually get them to the tailgate of my truck by saying, "Before I go up and measure your roof and look around, I've got a couple of things I'd like to show you over here ... just so you'll know what I'm talking about when you see them listed **on the estimate that I'm going to leave with you.**" (Hopefully, I just lowered their anxiety level, opened their ears, and focused them on what I was about to say instead of worrying about how they were going to avoid signing something when I try to get them to make an immediate decision.) And I head to the rear of my truck, immediately dropping the tailgate. Then I take some things out of my tool box, a one-foot piece of Drip Edge, a one-foot piece of E-6, a one-foot square piece of Ice and Water Shield, and a one-foot piece of Shingle Vent II or Snow Country ridge vent.

I've already looked at their roof enough to determine if they already have Drip Edge installed, or if they have crown molding going up the rakes. Most of the time I already know if they have valleys, skylights, chimneys, ridge vents, or other ventilation, and I know if they have soffit vents.

First, I show them the Drip Edge and explain why they need it and why we use it. Then I do the same with the E-6, stressing that, "The companies who care enough to put anything behind your gutters, usually install standard Drip Edge there, but that dog won't hunt." Then I tell them why that's not good and why E-6 is better. "Now, when you see Drip Edge and E-6 listed **on the estimate that I'm going to leave with you**, you'll know what I'm talking about."

Then I explain about Ice and Water Shield while showing them the sample, letting them feel that it's sticky on the back. And I tell them where and why we install it.

Now it's time for one of my big selling points. I pull a couple of 3-tab shingles from inside my bed, lay one along the edge of my tailgate, and explain to the customer why turning a 3-tab shingle backwards for starter is a terrible thing to do. "Most companies do it this way, but that's only because they don't know any better. Roofers have been doing it that way for years." Then I pull out a starter strip, show them the difference, and explain the benefits of using them, "I don't know why other companies don't use them, but most of them don't. It's just crazy, but like I said, they've been doing it the other way for so long, they just don't know any better. Hell, we were using the 3-tabs for starter too until we learned better a few years ago. The other guys may catch on some day … and then I'll have to find something else to brag about." I'll say that with a chuckle.

Next, I show them the piece of ridge vent and explain how the "lip and baffle" system creates an "area of negative air pressure at the ridge, just like an airplane wing creates lift, and it literally sucks the heat and humidity out of your attic … if you have somewhere for fresh air to get in. It has to be able to draw from somewhere. Let's see if you have that." And I head for their house to look at their soffit. Once there, I explain the bottom-to-top air flow. Then I head to the side of the house. "Of course, if you have gable vents on the ends, that's gonna screw everything up." If they do have gable vents, I'll explain why they have to cover them up from inside to allow the ridge vent/soffit vent combination to work properly. "So now, when you see Drip Edge, E-6, Ice and Water Shield, special starter shingles, and ridge vents that have the 'lip and baffle' *on the estimate that I'm going to leave with you*, you'll know what I'm talking about."

I spend a lot of time educating them on ventilation, and at some point, I'll slip in the little story about the last Professional Roofers Advisory Council meeting I attended and how much of that time was spent talking about ventilation, mold and mildew. "None of us paid any attention to stuff like that until a few years ago. Hell, most of the people in the roofing business still don't, but it's important. I try to stay up on stuff like that. I attend the classes, talk with industry people from the factories and manufacturers and distributors, and the experts over at the National Roofing Contractors Association. Roofing is just like anything else. *As technology improves, they come up with new and better ways to do things. I work hard to stay up on it."*

I train my new salesmen, who haven't had the opportunity to build their own resume of things like that to talk about, to use me. They can say, "We've got a guy in our company who is a member of the Professional Roofers Advisory Council and several other groups and organizations like that, and he stays up on the latest technology and advancements and stuff so that he can keep us all up to date on the new improvements in materials and installation techniques. He tours the factories where the materials are made, and he attends the International Roofing Expositions and things like that. Most companies don't have anyone like that, so we're lucky to have him." Of course, you should do your best to see that your salesmen tour factories and attend seminars and training classes and expos so they'll have their own resume to talk about. Remember, professionalism, professionalism, and professionalism. Doctors have to do it; lawyers have to do it; teachers have to do it; so why should a professional roofing salesman be any different?

Notice that I've gone over all of this educational stuff prior to getting up on the roof. If we aren't going to get along, or if they aren't interested in all those things (just the price), I should be able to see the homeowner's eyes glaze over and know something is wrong. If that's the case, I'd rather find out about it before I do all of that extra work, so that I can say, *"Now, obviously, since we're doing a lot more than the other companies, our price is going to be a little higher. Some folks don't really care about all of this stuff. They're selling their house or something and they really don't care. They just want the job done as cheaply as possible." And then I shut up and look right at them.* I won't continue with my presentation until we have that part straight. I want them to say something at least as committing as, "Oh, price won't be the only thing I look at." Or something to that effect.

Inspecting And Measuring

"Okay, well, I'm ready to get up there and take a look. Then I'll get in my truck and visit with my computer for a little while *and work up an estimate to leave with you*. That might take me thirty to forty-five minutes. You don't have to get somewhere, do you?"

Most often, they'll say no, so I'll add, "Good, then just go do whatever you have to do and I'll ring your bell when I'm finished."

> You're sitting in a doctor's office waiting room. The doctor peeks his head through the door, asks you to stand up, looks you over from across the room, writes out a prescription, and then says to the nurse, "Here's what's wrong with him, and here's his prescription." Then you're required to pay for the office visit and leave with your prescription.
>
> How confident do you feel with his diagnosis? How good do you feel about paying for the office visit? I'm guessing that the answer is "not very."
>
> You would at least like him to see you up close, right? You would like to be escorted back to the little room where the nurse can take your vital signs, right? You might even like the doctor to look in your ears, or down your throat, or examine that knee that was the reason you came to him in the first place, right?
>
> Okay, then how comfortable do you think a potential customer is going to feel about you walking around his house, looking up at his roof, and announcing, "I know what you need and how to deal with it."? I'm guessing the answer is "not very."
>
> Good! Now that we can agree on that, I suggest that you get up on your potential customer's roof and give it a thorough examination before you prescribe the cure.

Then, I get my ladder and get on their roof. I look around good, making sure to find at least three or four things to take pictures of. If I find some problems, I take pictures of those. If I don't, then I just take pictures of a pipe flashing, and the counter flashing on their chimney, and perhaps a shot of algae growing on their roof. I want to impress them with pictures. If there are problems on their roof, the pictures let me show them, instead of just telling them about it.

When I get back to my truck, I print out the estimate or estimates, along with the color pictures I took, and put them all into a nice folder with whatever sales material I want to leave. I may include some brochures on the shingles, and some material about our company. I always include a copy of our license and insurance.

Back To The Door

I often have a good laugh about a new salesman's second trip to the door. If he hasn't done a good job of letting the customer know that he is going to leave an estimate with them, thereby lowering the customer's anxiety level, he may be greeted with the situation that I'm sure you're all familiar with: the customer coming to the door, and cracking it three inches with a hand glued to the handle to prevent it from opening any further. They don't want the salesman to get in, and they don't want to "expose" themselves to him without the protection of the glass or screen between them. They may even stick their hand through the gap to take the estimate from him. I don't have that problem—at least not often. When I do, I know how to get them to open that door ... and open their ears, and open their minds.

I have the folder in my hand, closed, with the color photographs on top of it where they can see them. I make sure not to have a pen in my hand, and hopefully not one in their view at all. "Whew, well, I finally got 'er done. I only want to point out a couple of things *before I leave this estimate with you.*" And then I begin to explain what is in the photographs. If they are still protecting themselves with the door, they will open it. I guarantee it.

"Would you like to come in?"

"I'd better not. I've been up on your roof and I've got tar and stuff on my shoes. Besides, this will only take a minute. I've just got a couple of things to point out *before I go.*"

I show them the photographs. If I found problems, I show them those photos and explain them. If not, if I only took pictures of the pipe flashings and counter flashings, then I tell them, "When you see 'soil pipes' on my estimate, here's what I'm talking about, the pipes that vent your bathrooms and such. And when you see 'counter flashing' listed on the estimate, this is what I'm talking about, the metal around your chimney that you can see. Of course the step flashing and other flashings are hidden, but here's where they are."

They usually pay very close attention at this point. I open the folder and flip through the pages without taking them out of the folder. "I've put some things in here for you to look at when you have time: a copy of our license, our worker's comp insurance and our liability insurance, and my certificates that I put in there to make you think I know what I'm talking about (chuckle). I've also put in some information about our company, some general information on how to compare apples to apples, which of course is supposed to show you that we're great and all of the other guys are crooks (chuckle). I also put in some information on the kind of shingles that I think you should consider."

Then I take out the estimate, and say, "Here's the estimate. You'll see that I've listed out all the things I showed you out at my truck: the removal of the existing shingles, the Drip Edge, the E-6, the Ice and Water Shield, the ridge vents, and of course the cleaning up and hauling away of the debris. And here's the price." I point to the price on the bottom of the estimate. Then I close the folder quickly and hand it to them. "Do you have any questions ***before I take off.***"

If they don't, I close with, "***Okay then, get some other estimates, but make sure to do a good apples to apples comparison.*** My cell phone is listed about five hundred places in there, so call me if you have any questions." And I smile, shake their hand, and leave.

At this point, I want them to be thinking, "What a nice guy ... and he knows what he's talking about. I like him."

What Comes Next

In Stroudsburg, Pennsylvania, it would be some jackleg, showing up and counting the shingles from the ground to do his measurements, writing his estimate on the back of his business card, or giving it to the customer verbally. That's what most often happened (as I heard from many customers later), and that's why my closing ratio there was over 75 percent.

In the Washington, D.C. metro area, it's very different. Many of the salesmen from other companies who come out will chat with the customer, mostly about why they should upgrade to a more expensive shingle, and then do a decent estimate … by hand mostly. Some of them will leave without giving an estimate, so their office can type one up and send out a very nice presentation folder in a few days. They will probably have a flip chart, or a long drawn out sit-down presentation to go over. Most of it will be about their company. Then they'll spend a long time confusing the customer with the various (tedious) differences in warranties. And then they'll serve me up the job on a silver platter by trying to close the customer on the first visit. If they're good, really good, they may succeed. But I'll still get the job over 45 percent of the time. And that's not bad. I can live with that.

Of course, it's not all that unusual for the customer to stop me before I even get to my truck and want to sign a contract. When they do, I will almost always ask, "Don't you want to get some other estimates, or at least take some time to think it over?"

> Stroudsburg, PA, 2005. I did the unthinkable. I forgot an appointment. Kathy was on vacation and we were tripping all over each other to survive without her, and I simply forgot that I had an appointment. The customer called, and he wasn't a happy camper. He gave George an earful. I waved George off. I didn't want to take the call. George told the man that he would get in touch with me and have me call him.
>
> I waited ten minutes and called the customer, throwing out rapid-fire apologies before he could yell at me. "That's just not like me. I wish I had some excuse, but I don't. I just plain forgot about our appointment. I'm very sorry."
>
> "Well, are you going to come out here or not?"

He still didn't sound happy, and I wasn't looking forward to driving through the state park and up the mountain … way up the mountain, to give an estimate to someone who was already pissed at me. "Sure, if you still want me to. I wouldn't blame you if you didn't. When do you want me there?"

"How quick can you get here?"

I winced. "It's probably going to take me well over an hour to get up the mountain and find your house."

"I'll be here. Just try not to forget this time."

I looked at George and he was laughing his ass off. He knew exactly what I was thinking. I finally shrugged and headed out the door, telling George, "Oh well, I'm going to take a little joy ride up the mountain."

When I found the house and got the customer outside, I apologized again. Then I did my regular presentation, gave him the estimate and left. When I got out of the little lake community and back to the main road (which was no bargain of a road itself), I tried to call the office, but I didn't have cell service. I was halfway down the mountain when my phone notified me that I had a voice mail. Actually, I had three, all from George, urging me to turn around and go back to see the guy; he wanted to sign a contract. So that's what I did.

I like to tell this story when a salesman gets a lead that's a long way from the office and doesn't want to "waste his time" driving out there without calling the customer first and "feeling him out." My "feel" for this guy wasn't the warm fuzzies for sure, but I still made the sale.

12

Closing The Sale

The 90% Rule

I believe that 90% of all problems on a roofing job are created at the point of sale. Therefore, I also believe that 90% of all problems on a roofing job can be prevented at the point of sale. All it takes is for the salesman to recognize the potential problems and address those with the customer. If the customer knows what to expect, then they are not upset if it happens.

The real closing takes place after the contract is signed. I've seen many salesmen get a call from a customer to whom they gave an estimate, run out, pick a color and style of shingle, sign the contract and leave within fifteen minutes. Big mistake!

I have had salesmen (and even one owner) tell me that the reason they don't want to go back to the truck to reprint the contract when last minute changes are made is that they are afraid the customer, given that extra time to think, may back out of the deal. I always have to laugh at that one. When I stop laughing, I most often reply, "If that's what you're worried about, then the customer wasn't sold to begin with."

When Marty and I were partners in a small roofing company, he also had his own company, and we were working the same storm, but on different sides of a large lake. I knew most of his salesmen and was friends with several of them. One night one of his salesmen called me, bragging, "I just signed eleven contracts today. I blew your record away."

I congratulated him. The next day, I was meeting with Marty out in the field and I asked him to let me know how many of those customers canceled before their job was done. He said, "Hell, Neal, four of them

dy canceled. I'm going to have a long talk with that salesman
out not taking time to really close his deals."

The Good, The Bad, And The Ugly

I call what I do The Good, the Bad, and the Ugly. I have even typed out
some of it, and I include it in every presentation folder that I give out at
the time of the estimate. It explains many of the bad things that can happen during a roofing job. But, at the time of closing, I go over those things
again … and many more. "Mr. Homeowner, I hope you read the sheet
that I put in your folder called 'The Good, the Bad, and the Ugly,' but
even if you did, I want to go over some things with you. These are the
things that the other companies won't tell you. They only like to talk
about the Good. Here are some of the Bad and the Ugly."

1. Our production manager is going to call you and give you the pro-
    jected delivery date of the materials, but don't be mad if she doesn't.
    She's good, but sometimes things just get crazy and she forgets.

2. You've picked a fairly common color and style of shingle. It's usually
    in stock at several of the supply houses we order from, so it shouldn't
    take too long to get them out here. But, as sure as I say that, every
    darn supplier in town will be out of that color and style and they'll all
    have it on backorder. That probably won't happen, but don't be
    totally shocked if it does. It just happens sometimes.

3. If you get a call saying that the materials will be here on Thursday,
    don't be surprised if the supply company's truck breaks down or gets
    in a traffic accident on the way to your house. It happens sometimes.

4. If you get a call saying that the crew will be here the following morn-
    ing to start your job, don't be surprised if they don't show up. They
    might not get finished with the job they're doing the day before,
    because they ran into a lot of bad wood or something. Their vehicle
    might break down, or they might get in a traffic accident on the way
    over here, or the crew foreman's wife will go into labor in the middle

of it when the rain stopped. I was just a salesman then, but they were my customer.) We'll fix it and we'll accept responsibility for any interior damages it causes. Of course, we'll expect you to help minimize the damage by using towels or a trash can, moving furniture, and that kind of thing. Like I said, the chances of you having a leak are small, but it could happen, so don't panic if it does.

17. You've hired the right company to do your job. Any company looks good when everything goes right. But we shine the brightest when things go wrong. If something goes wrong, you can rest assured that we'll be right here with you to make it right.

Now, I've prevented 90% of the reasons that customer's get upset. I've warned them that bad things can happen, and that they shouldn't panic or get mad if they do. Most often, when something does happen, the customer will call me and say with a chuckle, "Neal, remember when you told me that a ladder might fall over and break a window … well, it just happened." Had I not warned them about things like that, they would have called me in a total panic.

Also, imagine the customer's delight when nothing does go wrong. When I hold out my hand for that final check, I often hear, "You know, you had me convinced that something bad was going to happen during the job and I was just waiting for it. But everything went without a hitch." To that, I'll laugh and say something like, "I'm sorry about that, but I've been in the business long enough to see just about everything go wrong that can. I've learned that it's better to prepare you for the worst and hope for the best."

> Lorton, Virginia, 1999. I sold a man a complete siding job. It was winter (that was the longest season I worked, well into spring) and I was in Texas for the Christmas holidays. The crew that was given the job was an old Greek man and his Hispanic helper (much too small a crew for that size job). There was snow everywhere and it was cold. They didn't work at all for days at a time, and when they did they only put in a couple of hours. They never should have been given the job to do in those conditions. Needless to say, the customer's property was a mess

throughout the holidays. He called me on my cell to complain. I called the office manager and he called the crew. Then I called the customer back and told him of my phone call to the office. And then I apologized and told him sadly that it would surprise me if my calls did any good. "It's the holidays, the weather is terrible, and I'm out of state. I don't know what else I can do, and I'm not going to bullshit you about it."

When I got back to Virginia after the holidays, I made a beeline to that customer's home. It was still a mess, and the quality of the work sucked. We finally had to get another crew out there to redo much of it, finish the job, and clean everything up.

Later, when I met with the customer to inspect the finished job and collect the final payment, he handed me the check while standing in his front yard and asked me, "Neal, you don't have to tell me if you want to, but I'm really curious about how much money you make in a year."

I didn't know why he wanted to know, so I was fairly ambiguous. I grinned and said, "I make pretty good money, probably a lot more than I'm worth. Why?"

He shook his head. "No, regardless of how much they pay you, it isn't enough. Virtually everything that could go wrong on a job did on this one. Yet, I'm not mad at you or your company, and you've got my final payment in your hand. Do you know why that is?"

I just shrugged and waited for him to tell me. Then he said, "It's because I trusted you. You warned me that things never go according to plan. And I never had any doubt that you were going to make everything right. It never crossed my mind that I was going to get stuck with a half-assed job. No company can possibly pay someone enough who is capable of instilling that kind of trust and confidence in their customers."

I got choked up as I shook his hand and thanked him for saying so … and assured him one more time that I was just a phone call away if he had any problems.

The Contract

If you look at a sales contract as a way to commit the customer to a deal, stop doing that. The purpose of a roofing sales contract is to protect the company. It may help a little if the customer decides not to pay, but often not. Most roofing sales contracts are not legally binding documents in the state they are being used in. Oh sure, they have a bunch of legal wording on them, but think about it, have you ever seen an attorney draw up an agreement, even for the simplest deal, that you could fit on the front and back of a letter size piece of paper and still leave most of the front side open to write or type the specifics of the job. No, I didn't think so. I haven't either.

A roofing sales agreement's main purpose is to show that there has been a "meeting of the minds" between you and the customer about what you're going to do to his home. If you're not specific, if many of the details of the job are only verbal and not outlined in the contract, then you're right back to a "who said what" position.

It never ceases to amaze me how many salesmen are too lazy to rewrite the contract when they get back out to the customer's home to close a deal. I don't have that problem, and neither do my salesmen, since we don't use our contract as an estimate. Our estimate forms don't even have a place for a signature on them. I did that on purpose.

The contract should list what you're going to do, what materials you're going to use, and any specific things that you and your customer talked about. It should specify the brand and color of the shingles, the color of the drip edge and E-6, the color and kind of ventilation, and the color of spray paint that will be used to paint the soil pipes (if any).

It should also specify things like how many layers are going to be removed, how bad decking will be handled, and how much additional charge per sheet it will cost the customer if you have to replace some of it. It should specify where Ice and Water Shield will be installed, what weight felt will be installed, and other such details. A simple line such as "Customer will be responsible for realignment of satellite dish" can save many upset customers and arguments later.

Nothing should be added to the contract later without having all of the copies together, so that all copies are exactly alike. And any changes or additions should be initialed by both parties.

The back of the contract (or at least most of it) is used to further protect the company. To make the customer feel good, we say something like: "All

_ed by Company will be completed in a good and workman-
_ind will meet or exceed industry standards."

Then we list things that we've been burned on in the past and let the customer know that he shouldn't try to burn us like that:

1. Company is not responsible for damage to the interior of the home sustained as the result of the reasonable and normal roofing process. Such damage includes, but is not limited to, such things as plaster falling, nail pops, pictures and/or mirrors falling off of walls, ceiling fans falling, or any other damage caused by pounding on the roof, or bundles of shingles being moved around or dropped onto the roof deck.

2. Company is not responsible for damage to personal belongings in the attic caused by dust, dirt, or roofing debris falling inside the attic during the reasonable and normal roofing process.

3. Company is not responsible for delays caused by acts of God, labor strikes, material shortages, or governmental actions that fall outside the control of Company.

4. Company is not responsible for minor denting or scratching of gutters.

5. Company is not responsible for minor cracking of driveway due to the weight of the truck/trailer used to collect and haul away roofing debris.

And the list goes on and on for as much room as you have to squeeze it in. Obviously, the longer you are in business and the more unreasonable customers you deal with, the longer the list will grow. The customer should be required to initial the back of the contract.

Cancellations

Customers cancel contracts. That's life. Deal with it. They suffer buyer's remorse, or the wife got in a car accident shortly after signing, or they got audited by the IRS the day after signing, or they died five hours after signing. And on, and on, and on.

The buyer's remorse is the only one of those that you can do something about. For me, the other things don't usually result in a canceled contract. They result in a postponed starting of the job. Remember, my customers signed with me because they like me, they trust me, and I didn't pressure them. It's not unusual for one of them to call me and tell me that this or that happened, and ask, "Can we put this off for awhile so that we can make sure we have the money available to pay you?" But it is unusual for them to say, "I want to cancel." I have earned their trust by that point, so they feel that they can confide in me. I like that, and I'll do everything in my power to show them that their trust wasn't misplaced. "Judy, tell me the truth now. Do you need me to give you the deposit back to help you through this? If you do, just say so. I will be happy to do that for you. I want to be your roofing guy, whether it's this month, or two years from now." And I'm not just saying that. I mean it (even if I know I'm not going to be around and that some other salesman is going to get the deal). You must develop that level of caring about your customers.

In Indiana in 1996, I signed a nice deal with a customer. Everything went fine until the materials were delivered. Then I got a call from him. He sounded sad and dejected, and timid about telling me what had happened.

"Neal, I don't know if you can help me, but I'm in a jam. I need to find some way to get out of this deal." When I asked him what happened, he explained, "You know that I'm an accountant and that I work out of my house. My largest client is a contractor and he was here this morning and saw the shingles in my driveway and your sign in the yard. He told me, 'If my roofing work isn't good enough for you, then your accounting work isn't good enough for me.' And he threatened to stop doing business with me. Is there any way you can help me. I can't afford to lose him as a client."

I told him that I'd let him out of the contract if he'd pay the supply company's restocking fee on the materials. He agreed, and I had the materials picked up. Over the next several weeks, he referred me to four new customers, and I got all four of those jobs.

But caring about your customers is not the only reason to let them out of contracts without a big hassle. There is another much more compelling reason: They don't want to do business with you.

When a roofing company accepts a small deposit (or none at all), orders materials, and sends out labor crews to do the work, they are issuing that customer credit … a lot of credit, and without doing a credit check or (except for the salesman) even meeting the customer.

How comfortable should you feel about issuing credit to a person, and spending your money on their behalf, if they don't like you (or perhaps even hate you) and they don't want to do business with you? It's a reasonable assumption that they are going to be difficult to please. They are going to pick your work apart. They are not going to like anything, from where the supply company set the materials, to the quality of the work. They'll want a third party to check your work. Then they'll want to wait to pay you until after it rains a few times to see if the roof leaks. Every minor problem will be magnified by a hundred. And in the end, you'll be lucky if you ever collect on the job.

You would think that only an idiot would want to put himself through all of that. But that's not the case. I've seen otherwise very intelligent owners argue with a customer and threaten to sue them if they try to cancel a contract.

I have stood in John's office and listened to cursing matches between him and a customer who wanted to cancel. When the phone call was over, I warned John, "Okay, but you're going to handle this deal from now on. I don't want any part of it. Before it's over, you'll be sorry that you didn't let her out of that measly little $3,500 siding contract. It's going to cost you a lot more than that in aggravation, even if you manage to collect the full balance, which I doubt is ever going to happen." Of course, after months of hassles, many more cursing matches on the phone, many trips out to her house to fix things that didn't really need to be fixed, John never did collect the full balance.

John is an otherwise very intelligent man. It just rubs him and other owners, sales managers, and salesmen raw to let someone cancel. I don't like it when people cancel, but I get over it a lot quicker and with less pain and mental anguish than the alternative, which could last for months.

13

Sales Tidbits

The Drive By

I am amazed at how many companies give "drive-by" estimates. The salesman gets a lead, drives to the customer's house, works up an estimate, and leaves it in the customer's mailbox. I'm also amazed at how those companies manage to stay in business as long as they do. Their expenses usually surpass their cash flow eventually, because they're selling for cash flow, not for profit.

Most of them do generate a large cash flow. The only way to sell a lot of roofs with drive-by estimates is to have the lowest price. What else is there for the customer to base his decision on? He doesn't know anything about the company that the estimate doesn't tell him, and he doesn't understand most of that. But he does understand the price.

> I was sitting in a roofing company's office in southern Virginia. It was my first hour of a three-day consulting job. There were five of us in a tiny room. I didn't know any of them except the owner. When he introduced me to the others, he didn't tell me their positions, only their names.
>
> After I'd given them the ten-minute synopsis of who I am and what I'm all about, the owner asked me, "What do you think of giving drive-by estimates … you know, leaving them in the mailbox without talking to the homeowner?"
>
> I chuckled. "If I catch one of my salesmen doing that, I'll fire him on the spot."
>
> The owner pointed to one of the other men in the room and said, "He sold well over a million dollars worth last year doing it that way."

I looked right at the salesman and said, "If I was his boss, and he refused to stop doing drive-bys immediately, I'd fire him on the spot."

I'm not sure why (wink), but the look on that salesman's face indicated that he wouldn't be opposed to taking me out behind the woodshed.

By the way, that was the same owner who, within five minutes of meeting me for the first time, told me that his company had done over seven million in sales the previous year and he didn't make any money. Enough said?

Follow-Ups

I always try to practice what I preach. When I can't (or don't want to), I try to be honest about it. This is one of those times. I teach my salesmen to follow up with customers after giving estimates, but I personally never do that.

I'm not a "salesman". I close deals by gaining the trust and respect of the homeowner, not by "selling" him. I don't handle rejection well. A homeowner never has the opportunity to reject me because I never ask for their business. They can't say no to a question that I don't ask. If they don't call me back to do business, they have said to me, "I don't like you, trust you, or respect you enough to do business with you." At least that's how I take it. They have rejected me. The thought of calling them up and giving them a chance to reject me again is revolting to me. I just can't force myself to do it. So I never have. My closing ratio would go up if I did. (I'm not an idiot. I know that it would.)

I have done something though, which was suggested to me by Lee Collins, a dear friend and a good roofing salesman (who now runs a multimillion dollar roofing office). He did it, and it worked for him, so I tried it. After giving an estimate, he would write the customer a brief note and mail it to them. The note would say something like: "Thank you for inviting me out to meet with you. I enjoyed meeting you [add 'and your family' if you did meet them]. If you have any questions about the estimate, or just questions in general, please do not hesitate to call me."

If you write the note soon enough after meeting them, you will often have some little tidbit to add to the note to make it personal, something about the antique car in their garage, or their sick mother, or their new grandbaby. Customers often mention that note when I meet with them to sign the contract. I don't know if they would have signed up anyway, but the fact that some of them mention the note is enough reason to do it.

I do teach my salesmen to follow up with the customers by phone a week or two after giving them an estimate. In fact, I insist that they do. Otherwise they well never know if the customer chose someone else over them, or why. They need that feedback, and so does the office.

When challenged on this point, I simply respond, "If your goal is to be as good as me, your goal isn't lofty enough. I want you to be better than me, to enjoy more success than me, and to make more money than I do. (Many of the guys I've trained have become much better than me.) So, in this instance, *do as I say, not as I do*. Besides, RHIP (rank has its privileges), so get over it."

Pictures

The contract is a great way to protect the company, but there is another, equally valuable tool available to your salesmen. They are at customers' homes, with their digital cameras hanging from their necks. They need to open their eyes and focus on things that might cause disputes between the customer and the company later. To help you understand the importance of this, I will need to delve back briefly into the realm of psychology.

We all get desensitized to things over time, whether it's violence on TV, or seeing our spouse naked for the eighty-five thousandth time (I'll try to keep mine from reading this part). It just happens. Believe it or not, this desensitization is a significant factor and plays a huge role in many disagreements between customers and contractors. Vick White, a district manager for Wendy's, once explained to me how the phenomenon affected the restaurant business. And he gave it a name; he called it a "skatoma". (I have no idea how to spell it. I've tried to look it up, but was unable to come close enough to get help from spell-check or my digital dictionary. It always pisses me off that I am expected to know how to spell something in order to look it up. If I new how to spell the damn word, I wouldn't need the dictionary.) Anyway, he called it a skatoma.

A manager of a restaurant walks through his dining room and notices a stain on the carpet. He's too busy to deal with it though, so he goes on with other things. He notices it again at closing time, but it's late and he's too tired to fool with it. He sees it again the next morning, but he's rushed to get the place opened up, and puts off dealing with it yet again. Every time he sees it without dealing with it, he becomes a little more desensitized to it. If this goes on long enough, he will stop noticing it altogether. When he walks through his dining room after that, everything looks normal. The stain has become normal. Vick White solves this problem by shuffling his assistant manager's around between stores, and having them write down everything they see that looks wrong, out of place, or in need of attention. That store's manager is required to address each item on the list within twenty-four hours.

So, how does that cause problems with our roofing customers? The answer is: In thousands of ways. A customer's gutters are all dented up, but he stopped noticing the dents long ago—until he started inspecting your work. He's paying attention now, looking for things. He sees the dents. In his mind, they weren't there before you did his roof, so your crew must have caused them. The same applies to the small cracks in his driveway, and the oil spots that his brother-in-law's car dripped on it the year before.

> McLean, Virginia, 2004. A week after we'd installed his new roof, an upset customer called the office. His painter told him that there was an area of his new roof that looked terrible, like the shingles were just thrown on the roof without even trying to line them up. He couldn't see that part of the roof from the ground. It was on the 2-story part and only a 4–12 pitch. His backyard sloped down drastically. He had crawled out of his window and peeked up there, and sure enough, there was a large area, ten feet by six feet, that looked really bad, shingles just tacked on in a random, helter-skelter manner.
>
> I went out there immediately. The customer wasn't home, but I put my ladder up in front and made my way to the upper back slope. Sure enough, the area was just like he'd described it. The rest of the roofing

job was perfect, so I was baffled. I called the foreman of the crew that had done the job. He insisted that he had done a final inspection and the roof was perfect. Finally, I had him meet me out there.

When the foreman arrived, he looked at the area and scratched his head. "Neal, there was a small dormer here when we did the roof. It was very small, and I don't know what it was for, but it was here, I swear it."

I called the customer at work and related what my crew foreman had said. He reacted harshly. "There's never been any dormer on that roof. You're roofer is lying to you."

"Sir, I've worked with him for a long time, and I can say with certainty that he would never have left your roof in this condition, and he would not lie to me about something like this. I'm sure that something has happened to your roof since we did the job."

"Well, you're full of shit and your roofer is full of shit, and you'd better get my f—ing roof fixed or I'll call the Better Business Bureau … and I'll sue your ass."

Finally, I called the salesman who'd sold the job and asked him about it. "I don't remember any dormer," he told me.

"Do you still have your pictures of the roof?"

He did. He drove over there and we looked at the pictures on his laptop. When I saw the one showing that area of the roof, I asked him to print it out for me. Then I apologized to my crew foreman and went back to the office. When I got there, I called the customer again. I know that I shouldn't handle customers like this, but there are customers and situations that I simply can't resist having a little fun with. I started off by saying something like, "I grilled my crew foreman again, and he still insisted that there was something on your roof when he did the job that isn't there now."

The customer went off on me again, this time even worse than the first time. He called me, my crew foreman, and our company every name in the book. When I was sure that he'd dug himself a deep enough hole, I asked him, "Oh, by the way, did you used to have a chimney on the back of the house?" When he confirmed that he'd just had one removed prior to us doing the roof, I said, "Well, sir, do you know what the hump behind a chimney is called?" He didn't, so I told him. "It's called a cricket. And without the chimney there, a cricket is no more than a small dormer looking thing. The guy who removed your chimney didn't remove the cricket until *after* we'd done the roof, and he didn't know how to put the shingles back afterward. Now, I'm sitting here looking at a picture of that cricket/dormer ... prior to us doing the roof. It's not there now. But I'm going to take it easy on you. I'm only going to charge you eight hundred dollars for fixing it—well, actually that's five hundred for fixing it, and three hundred for having to endure your arrogant foul-mouthed name-calling. Do you want us to fix it or not?" He paid the $800-or I should say his wife did.

Pictures have settled many disputes for me. Your salesmen should take a lot of them. They don't need to print them all. They can just upload them to their laptops and keep them handy. I've taken so many that I have to save them onto CDs periodically to free up space on my laptop. Every time I'm in a customer's home, before or after doing his roof, and he points out some areas where his roof has leaked in the past, I take pictures of the stains. Several times I've had customers try to blame us for old damage to get us to paint or replace drywall. I've had them try to blame us for gutter damage, dents in aluminum siding, broken vinyl siding, broken lighting rods and weather vanes. Pictures have settled many of those claims.

Surprises

As a consumer, I hate surprises, especially when they cost me more money. Try to avoid them. I have lost jobs because I've been honest with the customer about things like bad decking, when my competitors were not.

> Springfield, Virginia, 2003. I ran a lead and did my standard presentation, right up until the time I got on the roof. The decking was bad ... really bad. I almost fell through in several places, and I'm not a big guy. It was a small, simple roof (under 20 squares). Before doing my measuring, I went down my ladder and knocked on the customer's door. When he came outside, I explained, "I hate to tell you this, but I've got some bad news for you. You've got a lot of bad decking. I almost fell through your roof in several places. I don't know how much needs to be replaced, but I wouldn't be surprised if it all does. The cost of your job just went up by more than double."

The customer stared at me hard for several seconds before saying, "You're a f—ing liar. I've had three other companies out here and none of them said one word about my decking being bad."

Well, by this point in my book, I'm sure you know how I reacted. I knew I was right. "Mister, let me tell you something before I get in my truck and leave. Those other guys didn't tell you about your bad decking for one of two reasons: either they didn't get up on your roof, or they did, but they didn't want to risk losing the job because of having to include all of that decking in the price. But I can guarantee you this, if you read their contracts you'll find that there is a provision in there for how much they're going to charge you, over and above the contract price, to replace any bad decking they find. They aren't being honest with you. I am. So you deserve everything you get from them. Have a wonderful day." And I got my ladder and drove away.

Two days later, that guy called me. "I'm sorry for calling you a liar. I had a friend of mine that knows about roofing get up there and check my roof. He agreed with you. I want you to do my job."

"Thank you. I bare you no hard feelings, but I'm not going to do your job. I've seen how you can be, and I don't want your business. You'll have to find yourself another roofing company."

A week later, the guy called me again, practically begging me to do his job. I told him that I could not do business with him, but I would pass him to the owner of the company and let him make the final decision. John was in the office, so I quickly filled him in on the deal, strongly suggesting that we not do business with this guy. John took my advice.

The longer a salesman is in the roofing business, the more his "gut feel" for problem customers improves. Unfortunately, if a salesman is struggling and hungry, he will often ignore his gut. Owners never should.

Honesty is the best policy, even when it means losing a job here and there. Even if you're not sure that there is going to be an extra expense, but there is a good possibility of it, you should inform the customer up front. If something is going to look bad after the job is done, simply because of the construction of the house or other situation on their roof, tell them about it up front.

Oshkosh, Wisconsin, 2000. Many of the older homes in that area were two-story and had steep roofs, with cedar shingles as the bottom layer, installed over spaced lathing, not solid decking. Most of them had three to six layers of composition shingles installed over the top of the cedar shingles. In most cases the aluminum siding had been installed much later, or cut back during the installation of additional layers of shingles.

When all layers were removed, including the cedar shingles, new decking had to be installed. The insurance company most often picked up the tab, so it made for nice contract amounts for the roofing company, and didn't cost the homeowner anything.

The problem was that when you remove five, six, or even seven layers of shingles (especially when one of them is cedar shingles or cedar shakes), you have removed four to six inches of roofing. The siding was most often flush with the top layer, so when you only installed a little more than ½" of decking and shingles back, there was a terrible looking, ugly, ugly, ugly gap—sometimes as much as 4"—between the top of the shingles and the bottom of the siding.

After the job, customers would see the gap and go ballistic. It made the whole job, and their house, look terrible. After once such experience, I began explaining the situation to customers in advance, and showing them a Polaroid picture of a house we'd done previously and what the gap would look like. Bingo! Now they expected it, and there was no problem. I simply explained, "It's a siding problem, not a roofing problem. There is no way to avoid it. You'll just have to have someone come out here later and install something over the gap to hide it."

It's very difficult to look a customer in the eye and break bad news to them, especially before they have chosen you as their roofing company. However, the unpleasant possibility of losing the job is nothing compared to the unpleasantness of doing the job and not getting paid for it afterward. Be honest with them up front, and then let them make the decision whether or not to hire you to do their job.

The Art of Collecting

Make no mistake about it, collecting is an art. I'm not sure why, but many salesmen are shy about holding out their hands for the final check. I have found that collecting is a lot easier if I start the process during the close. If you wait until the job is completed, then it's almost like, "Oh, and by the way … I need to get that final check from you." That is awkward at best.

Every minute that goes by after the job is done, and before it is collected, increases the difficulty of collecting the final payment. A neighbor comes over and says, "I sure don't like the way that looks." Or a brother-in-law, the drunken ex-roofer, stops by and tells your customer, "I wouldn't pay the bastards until after it rains a few times, to make sure it doesn't leak." Simply getting out there as quickly as you can after the job is complete reduces the odds of something like that happening.

When I'm involved in my "close after the close," which is what I call the litany of things I go over with the customer after the contract has been signed, I make sure to bring up the payment of the final check. I usually do it this way:

"And then, once the job is completed, I'll come out and inspect it. I'll go around and pick up the small stuff that the crew missed during cleanup, and then, if the job passes my inspection, it will be time for the fun part. That's when I get to hold out my hand for the final check. You know, I don't get paid until the job is done and you're happy with it. Then you pay me, so that's the fun part for me."

Then, after the job is done, I call the customer and say, "Are you going to be home later?" If they say yes, I ask, "How's our new roof look?" I'm fishing here. I'm trying to find out if there is a problem that I should know about and deal with before I get on to asking for that final check. If they don't mention any problems, I continue with, "Okay then, I'm going to drop by and do my final inspection. If everything looks good on the roof, I'll check around the house to see if the crew cleaned up good. If everything looks okay, it will be time to get to the fun part … the part where I get to hold out my hand for the final check."

Later, when I get to their house, I'll knock on the door and tell them, "I'm going to take a look at the job and check the cleanup. You'll know if everything looks okay to me, because I'll knock on your door again with a big smile on my face and my hand out."

I've mentioned collecting that final check from them three or four times, and made a joke out of it each time. So there is no surprise or embarrassment when I knock on the door again and say, "Everything looks great. I picked up a few things that the crew missed, but I'm sure they were worn out by the time they finished up, and it was probably getting a little dark by then. Now it's time to get to the fun part. If you don't have a pen, I keep about two hundred of them in my truck for emergencies." By then, they know full well what I'm referring to, and we usually have a good laugh about it. "If you screw up and put an extra zero or two on the end there, it won't make me or the company mad." Or, "Just make the check out to me … that's N-E-A-L." And then I laugh and tell them that I'm just kidding.

As you can see, I make a big joke out of the collecting, but I start that early, even before the ink is dry on the contract. If you've already talked about them writing the final check a few times, and joked about it, then there is no need to be shy about asking for it.

I equate collecting the final check to a teenager taking a girl to her door after a first date. It's awkward. She doesn't know if he's going to try to kiss her. He doesn't know if she'll let him kiss her. But, if they'd talked about it in advance (even though it would have taken the suspense out of it), it would be easier.

> *"Will you go to the movies with me this Saturday?"*
> *"Yes, that would be nice. I'd love to."*
> *"Great, then I'll pick you up at six-thirty. We'll watch the movie and then I'll drive you home. When we get there, I'll walk you to the door and kiss you. How does that sound?"*
> *"That sounds wonderful."*
> *"Great, I'll see you then, and I'll really be looking forward to that kiss."*

Okay, so that ruined the spontaneity, but it did remove all of the guesswork on both their parts. They both knew what was coming when he walked her to the door, and they had reached a "meeting of the minds" about it in advance … not very romantic, but effective.

When it comes to collecting, I could care less about romantic. I'm interested in effective.

The Whiners

Roofing salesmen can be the biggest whiners in the world. Most often, the best of them are the worst whiners.

"Bill is getting all the good leads."

"That's funny. The other guys were in here saying the same thing about you last month."

"The production manager keeps screwing up my orders."

"Okay, then you can sit in her chair for the next month and see if you can do any better."

"The crews never follow the instructions on the work orders."

"Hmm, then perhaps you should make a special effort to get out to your jobs earlier and go over things with them to make sure they understand what you want."

"I can't collect the final check on this big job because they won't get out there and fix that little problem."

"I understand. If I were you, I'd be in here first thing in the morning, grab one of the guys off of the crew and some materials and take them over there ... and don't leave until they've got the problem corrected."

"We're out of samples in the sales office."

"That's terrible. You'd better get over to the Roof Center or ABC and pick some up. Get enough for everyone. On your way, call the Elk rep, the GAF rep, and the Certainteed rep, and tell them all that we can't sell their shingles without samples."

"The production manager didn't notify me that my job was starting this morning."

"Yeah, I hate it when that happens. You should probably keep a closer eye on the production board so that you'll know when your jobs are getting close, and then call her every morning just to double check with her."

"I just lost a $40,000 job to Acme Roofing. Their estimate was two thousand dollars less than mine. Our prices are just too high."

"One of two things must have happened. Either the customer wasn't interested in the quality, just the price, or you didn't do a good job explaining what we do differently and why they should pay the higher price. Which of those do you think it was?"

"Our brochure sucks. Some of the other companies have nicer ones."

"Yeah, I don't like ours that much either. Why don't you design a better one and I'll have a look at it. If yours is better, I'll have some printed up."

"Bill got one of my referral leads and sold it. It was a $45,000 job."

"Damn! I'll do my best to find out how that happened, and I'll talk to Bill and see if I can arrange some way for you to earn a piece of it. But it happens. It always has, and it always will, despite everything we do to try to prevent it. That's just the way it is."

And on, and on, and on, and on. Expect it. Prepare yourself to deal with it, and let your guys know early on that you've been in their shoes and experienced everything that they are going to experience. A perennial favorite of mine is, "That's why you make the big bucks." I like to save, "If it gets too much for you, I hear that McDonald's is hiring," for the really special occasions.

Absentee Salesmen

In a perfect world, we would never roof a job when the salesman can't be there to baby-sit it. Unfortunately, we don't do business in a perfect world. Regardless of how hard you try to avoid doing it, you will roof a job while the salesman is on vacation, sick, or otherwise unavailable. It often happens simply because the production manager forgets (or was never told) that the salesman would be unavailable. She leaves him a voice mail about his job starting and doesn't know until afterward that he never got the message. When it happens, expect problems ... and expect an unhappy salesman when he returns.

It's a fact of life that salesmen make promises to their customers that aren't put in the contract. I do it, and every salesman I've ever known does it. It may be something as simple as the customer requesting that the crew access the back of the house through this gate instead of that one because of a patch of new grass that he planted; or paying special attention to a trouble spot where the roof has leaked in the past. It might be something more urgent, like not doing the job on a particular day of the week or starting before a certain time.

Many of those things can be handled in the contract and in the special instructions to the crew, but they are often overlooked, even if they're in bold type and highlighted. In a busy production office, things like that get missed. It's just a fact of life. When they are missed, the customer is unhappy, and he takes it out on the salesman who made the promise. The job is more difficult to collect, the likelihood of referrals is reduced, and the salesman is unhappy.

When things like that happen, a call from you to the customer explaining what happened is sometimes enough to calm them down enough so they won't throw rocks at Bill when he shows up to collect. "We simply screwed up. It wasn't Bill's fault. Our production manager didn't realize that Bill was out of town." If Bill's absence caused a more serious problem, you showing up at the customer's house with Bill might help. Customers are usually impressed when the owner shows up to apologize in person.

Mooresville, Indiana, 1996. I told Marty that I would be going back to Texas for a few days. "Let me know a week ahead of time and we won't do any of your jobs while you're gone." So that's what I did. Of course, when I returned they had done one of my jobs. The customer was a therapist, and worked out of her home. All of her appointments were on Thursdays, so I had put in bold type everywhere on the paperwork: **Do the job any day but Thursday**. You know what day the job was done … Thursday, of course. Of the 99 jobs I sold that year, that was the only one that I wasn't able to collect in full.

When you roof a job while the salesman is unavailable, expect problems, and start preparing your list of apologies.

14

Fire Them

Wouldn't it be great if everyone we hired proved to be everything we'd hoped they would be when we hired them? Unfortunately, that is never the case. I don't believe in the theory, "throw a pile of crap against the wall and see what sticks," as many sales organizations do. I hire the people whom I think will have the best chance of succeeding, and the least chance of wasting my time. Still, I'm wrong about as often as I'm right ... sometimes more. Art Williams is fond of saying, "There is no test devised that can look inside the heart of a man or woman and tell whether they've got the goodies or not." I agree with that one hundred percent. Likewise, there is no manager that I know who can predict with any degree of certainty who will become successful and who will not. I know that I can't.

An unsuccessful salesman costs a company a lot more than the time wasted hiring and training him, especially if you keep him around too long. He wastes leads. Handing him one is almost as bad as throwing it in the trash ... sometimes worse. If he doesn't represent your company well, he gives the potential customer an unfavorable impression of you, one which may be shared with a friend, neighbor or relative later.

Unfortunately, what he costs you in leads and reputation is a mere drop in the bucket compared to some of the other bad things that will result from keeping an unsuccessful salesman around too long. If he's not doing well, his morale will be shot, and he will infect the other salesmen, even if not intentionally. Also, the other salesmen will see that you weren't serious when you explained about your expectations for them and that you wouldn't accept poor or even mediocre performance. The cliché is true: one rotten apple can spoil the whole barrel, even if it's not intentional. He may be a great guy, and he may be trying very hard, and you and everyone else may like him, but those aren't good enough reasons to keep him around.

Salesman X

Salesman X was one of my original A-Team at NVR. He was six-foot nine, if I remember correctly, and filled out his sturdy frame. He was a good-looking kid, but he knew more about roofing and construction than I would have preferred. He won Salesman of the Month three months in a row. Then, one week after presenting him with his third Salesman of the Month plaque and a special "Golden Turkey" trophy for winning three consecutive months, I fired him.

Why would I do that? I fired Salesman X for two major reasons, but both were seeds of the same problem: he was a weak salesman. He couldn't say no to a customer. He would agree to almost anything and promise almost anything to make a sale. That's how he managed to sell so many big jobs. The problem was that we couldn't live up to all of the promises he made. His customers didn't end up happy, and we had a terrible time collecting on his jobs.

I started off by teasing him in sales meetings about having so many "odd" things on his contracts. When that didn't have any effect, I counseled him privately and warned him that he had to stop it. He didn't.

Finally, I reached the end of my rope, called him in, and fired him. I liked him, so it wasn't easy, especially since he was an original member of the A-Team, but it had to be done.

Salesman Y

Salesman Y was another original member of the A-Team. I almost didn't hire him in the first place. He was very young, and a little too laid back for my taste. He was soft-spoken and hesitant to speak up, and he didn't have a pickup. He drove a small two-door Honda. But Salesman Y was intelligent and willing, and he seemed like a genuinely good person, honest, polite, and respectful. He was good at math and had great computer skills. So, I hired him.

Over the course of the next few months, everyone fell in love with Salesman Y, including me. He was a great guy. He didn't make as many sales as the other guys, but he tried hard. I had to buy him a fold-up ladder that would fit in his car, and I knew that was hurting his closing ratio. The D.C. metro area has a lot of tall roofs, and I was sure he couldn't get on the vast majority of them with the fold-up ladder. But Salesman Y managed to sell enough jobs to keep me from giving up on him.

A few months after joining NVR, he got married and had a baby on the way. Everyone at the company was elated for him.

Salesman Y had been with the company for well over half a year when he made the mistake that I couldn't let pass. He announced to the world that he wasn't committed to the job or to the company. Of course, he didn't come right out and say it in those words, but he might as well have.

I was in my office doing paperwork. I heard voices in the hall and recognized them as Salesman Y and one of the other members of the A-Team. I heard Salesman Y say, "I'm getting a new car."

The other salesman said, "That's great, what kind?"

"A Saturn."

"Oh, I hear they're really great cars, very reliable and they get good gas mileage."

I got up from my desk and peeked out into the hallway. "Salesman Y, could you come in here please?" When he came into my office, I told him to shut the door and have a seat. I rarely closed my office door, so Salesman Y suspected that he might be in trouble. I didn't keep him guessing. "Salesman Y, I love you, but you're fired."

Salesman Y's mouth dropped open. When he could speak, he asked, "Why? What did I do wrong?"

I stared at him hard and said, "One of the things listed under qualifications in the Monster.com ad that you responded to was 'have a pickup or be willing to trade into one within a reasonable time.' When I hired you, we had a long talk about dedication, and commitment. Do you remember those conversations?" He indicated that he did, so I continued, "I just heard you out in the hall saying that you're going to buy a new Saturn. I know that you can't afford to buy two new vehicles, so I can only assume that you're putting any plans to buy a truck on hold for awhile … a long while. Am I right?"

"There's no way I can—not with a baby on the way. I can't afford it."

"If you can afford a new Saturn, you can surely afford a used pickup, but it's a moot point now anyway. You've already let me know loud and clear how dedicated and committed you are to your job, and to this company. I won't have someone around here that isn't committed to becoming successful. Like I said, I love you, but you're still fired."

Needless to say, everyone in the company was devastated. They couldn't believe that I had fired Salesman Y. I heard them whispering, and cutting their conversations about it short when I'd walk in, but I didn't shy away from telling them why I'd done it, and that I'd do it again. "We're building something very special here, and we need special people to make it work, people who believe in what we're doing, people who want more than anything to be a part of it, dedicated people, committed people. I won't settle for people who just pay it lip service."

Salesman Z

Oshkosh, Wisconsin, 2000. Salesman Z was a good friend of mine. I'd known him for years, even before I got into the roofing business. He'd been a roofing salesman for many years before I met him in 1993. When I opened my own company in Oshkosh, he came to work for me.

A few months into the storm, Salesman Z wrote me a letter expressing his displeasure over a change I'd made to the commission structure. We had a written agreement, but I had found out later that the commission structure wasn't appropriate to the nature of the storm and the way the insurance companies were paying. I had called a sales meeting, explained the problem to all of my salesmen, and outlined the changes. It was fair, and none of them voiced any objections to the change. But now, two months after the change was instituted, Salesman Z had a problem with it.

I met with Salesman Z and we discussed it. At some point, Salesman Z pulled out his copy of our initial agreement and told me that I hadn't put the changes in writing, so they weren't valid. I stared at him in disbelief. I couldn't believe that he would pull that, not after verbally agreeing to the changes when I had presented them to the entire sales force.

Finally, I explained to Salesman Z that I was building a family, and that I wanted to build it with team players, people who wanted to be a part of the family and help the company grow and prosper so that we could all benefit from it. I hadn't made the changes out of greed, and Salesman Z knew and understood that. I'd done it for all of us, not to line my pockets. Then, I told him, "Salesman Z, I'm shocked and disappointed, but you obviously don't care about the team, so I'm going to sever our business relationship. (I couldn't fire him because he was a subcontractor.) And then I told him, "You've hurt me, so it's best that we take some time to let me get my emotions under control before we discuss how to settle up on the jobs you have pending. I want you to go make a list of what you think you have coming, and I'll do the same. Let's meet in two days and go over it. I want to end this thing in a way that will allow us to walk away still friends."

Two days later, Salesman Z took a seat in my office. I asked him, "Have you got the breakdown on what you think I owe you?"

"Yes, but I'd like to see yours first," he said.

I pulled the piece of paper out of my shirt pocket and handed it to him. "See if you think this amount is fair."

Salesman Z stared at the amount I'd written on the paper. After a long while, he looked at me with sad eyes. I thought he was going to start tearing up. "Neal, this is very … generous. It's a lot more than I have coming."

I nodded. "I know, but like I told you two days ago, I want us to part friends. The amount written down there is just money. Your friendship is more important to me than dollars. I'm not letting you go because of the money. I'm doing it for the health and well being of the team. You've made it clear that you don't want to be a team player, so I can't keep you around. But that doesn't mean that I don't want to keep you as a friend."

Salesman Z and I are still good friends today.

Throughout my thirty-plus years in management, I've had to fire a lot of people. I've most often managed to do it with respect and in a way that let the person maintain their dignity. I don't belittle them, but I don't bullshit them either. I don't patronize them, or make up flimsy excuses. If I'm firing them because they aren't any good at the job, I tell them so. I don't say, "We have to cut back on our overhead" or some other such nonsense. If they're no good at their job, they need to know it, so that they can look for a different kind of job. The biggest favor you can do for someone you're firing is tell them the truth about why you're doing it.

Don't get me wrong though, I'm human and I get mad. I've told people, "You're fired. Don't let the f—ing door hit your ass on the way out." But, in those instances, there was no doubt in their minds about why I was firing them, so there was no need for a sit-down discussion about it.

I have fired very few people over those years who I would avoid if I saw them in the mall or at a party. There are a few, but I would avoid those only because I still haven't gotten over what they did to get fired. It wouldn't be because I was ashamed of my behavior while firing them.

When you have to fire someone, do it with respect, but don't hand them a line of bullshit. Tell them the truth, so that they can evaluate why they got fired and make changes in their behavior … if they are so inclined. When someone has really upset you, firing them is best done after a cooling off period. Like revenge, firing someone is a dish best served cold.

15

The Extras

Someone is always coming up with new and exciting ways to increase closing ratios, especially roofing manufacturers and roofing suppliers. After all, they have a vested interest in helping their customers sell more roofs. The Bradco Supply rep has a vested interest in seeing that the companies who buy from him sell more roofs than the companies who buy mostly from ABC. GAF wants to help their preferred contractors sell more than the companies who sell mostly Certainteed products. Sometimes they come up with great ideas ... sometimes not.

Warranties

Roofing manufacturers have been playing with their warranties forever. Every one of them has come up with unique and interesting new ways to warranty their products. Some of them even warranty your installation, if you're one of their preferred contractors, if you use only their materials, if you use only their accepted installation techniques (which are often squirrelly to say the least), and if they inspect the job prior to issuing the warranty. Of course, those "special" warranties cost money. Manufacturers aren't going to increase their liability without increasing their revenue. That only makes sense.

You could spend an hour or more trying to explain the intricacies of the various warranties to a potential customer. I can just see the customer's eyes glazing over before the salesman is halfway through explaining all of the options. I already spend an hour, more often and hour and a half, with a customer, without even getting into warranties. I can't imagine adding even an extra thirty minutes to my presentation to cover warranties, let alone an hour.

Even without the manufacturer bearing some of the burden for the labor warranty, some roofing companies have fallen prey to the notion that offering a longer labor warranty than their competition is a great way to improve the closing ratio of their salesmen. Unfortunately for them, this is sometimes true. I have seen roofing companies go under, simply because they stayed in business long enough for their warranty liability to catch up with them. Some of them offer five and even ten year labor warranties. My question is: why?

What is the purpose of a labor warranty in the first place? Isn't it simply to protect the customer from faulty installation of the roofing materials? How long is a reasonable time to determine that?

In most markets, especially those with diverse weather patterns, two years is plenty of time to test the installation of a roofing job. If the shingles don't blow off in two years, and if the damn thing doesn't leak in two years, then the roofing materials were probably installed correctly. After all, it withstood two winters with no problems, and two summers, and the winds and rains of two springs. It withstood the mixed weather of two falls. If it does that, the roof was probably installed correctly. If it leaks after that, or if shingles blow off after that, isn't it reasonable to assume that something else happened to that roof to cause the problem?

From 1996 to present, the longest labor warranty I've given a customer is five years. I've given maybe as many as four of those (just because that was what it took to get the job, and it was clear that I wasn't going to talk the customer out of it). The rest were all two-year labor warranties. If you explain it right, a two-year labor warranty will make sense to most customers.

I have had customers actually call the office after hurricane Isabelle in 2003 and insist that we fix their roof for free after a tree fell on it due to the hurricane. They say. "But it's still under warranty."

When a customer takes his new car into the repair shop, he expects the dealership to duck their responsibility and charge him something for the repairs. The same holds true for his new computer, and his lawn mower, anything else he's purchased with a warranty, including his new roof. Sadly, we're used to finding out that warranties are worthless. If you plan to be in business for a long time in the same market, anything you can do to avoid telling a customer that your warranty doesn't cover his problem is worth doing. Your reputation is on the line. You don't want people out there saying that you don't honor your warranty, regardless of whether or not you were in the right for not doing so. The customer won't see it the way you do.

Extending your labor warranty just for "bragging rights" at the point of sale, increases the number of times when you have to tell a customer, "I'm sorry, but your problem isn't covered under the warranty."

> Shortly after joining NVR, I was riding in the truck with John Francis to look at a problem. We suspected that we were going to make a repair sale, since the roof in question was already out of warranty by almost a year.
>
> Upon arriving at the house and inspecting the interior damage and the roof itself, John said to me, "Damn, we didn't flash this chimney correctly." I didn't say anything. I wanted to see how John would handle that situation with the customer. I was impressed when John told the customer, "Obviously, your roof is out of warranty, but after looking at it, I can tell that it's our fault. We didn't do a good job on your chimney flashing. So, we're going to fix it at no charge." The homeowners thought John was a saint. They couldn't believe it. I couldn't believe it. I knew right then that John Francis was worth working for. I have related that story to dozens of potential customers when talking about warranties. I'm sure that they could sense on my face and in my voice that I was telling the truth.

A warranty is only as good as the company that issues it. They will either look for a way to get around honoring it, or they will look for a reason to make good on it. Which kind of company do you think has the best chance of developing a good reputation in the market?

> In early 1993, I was driving down I-35 in Dallas, Texas in my six-month-old 1992 Chevy pickup. I was going 65 miles an hour when it

died and wouldn't restart. I immediately called the dealership and they sent a wrecker to fetch my new pickup.

The next day, I received a call from the service desk, "Your pickup is fixed and ready for you to come and get." But when I got to the dealership, they explained, "It was normal carbon buildup. We took care of it for you. You only owe us $625.00 for the repairs." I was furious. I called Larry Stelk, my boss. He owned a used car wholesale business (among his bevy of business holdings) and I knew that he did a lot of business with that dealership. Of course, I called him from the service manager's office, after giving the service manager several pieces of my mind. I explained to Larry what they were trying to do to me. Larry told me not to worry about it, that he would call the owner of the dealership and get it taken care of. "Tell the service manager who I am and that I'm just about to call the owner of the dealership on your behalf." I related that to the service manager, and voila! The repairs magically fell under the warranty. I wasn't going to be required to pay a cent. Imagine that!

I won't buy anything, not even a part, from that dealership again. And if someone mentions that they are about to buy a new vehicle, I tell them that story, hoping that they won't buy from that dealership.

The longer your labor warranty, the more chance there is that your customer will call you with a problem that they expect to be covered by it, and the greater the chance will be that their problem is not your fault. Therefore, by extending your labor warranty, you are only increasing the number of times you have to tell a customer: "I'm sorry, but your problem isn't covered under the warranty." That will eventually destroy your reputation in the market, whether you were in the right or not. Don't create a situation where you have to do that. Set your labor warranty at a length of time to sufficiently test the quality of your installation. Then, if a problem occurs later that is your fault and for some reason just didn't show up during the warranty period, you'll be presented with the perfect opportunity to be the hero by fixing the problem for free.

Financing

"Damn, if I can offer to finance a new roof, the customer will pay my higher price without giving it a second thought. After all, he's only obligating himself to $40.00 per month, not facing the prospect of writing a couple of checks totaling $15,000.00."

I have sat through many, many hours of listening to reps from GE and other financing companies "explain" the roofing sales process to me. On those occasions when I manage to stay awake throughout their presentations, I understand how their pitch might hook some roofing people. But the devil is in the details, as is most often the case.

Oh sure, it sounds neat as hell. It only takes a few minutes on the phone to get a customer qualified. You'll get all of your money in a lump sum from the finance company when the job is completed. You'll be able to close a lot more deals. And on and on and on. One such finance salesman even had the audacity to explain to me how to sell a roof (even though when questioned about it, he finally had to confess that he'd never actually sold one). I don't mind sharing that he was a GE Financing rep … and an arrogant asshole.

While I was away on a long-term consulting job, one such salesman convinced John and Deryl to try the financing thing. What they found was about what I expected. The customers who were most attracted to the idea were the ones who couldn't qualify for the financing. When they got a customer accepted for the financing, they had to jump through a lot of hoops to get their money, and most often they couldn't get it in a timely manner because the customer wouldn't cooperate by signing all of the release forms after the job was finished.

When a customer calls your office for an estimate, he has already prepared himself mentally for spending the money. The price may be higher than he expected, but not usually high enough to alter his decision to get a new roof. By introducing him to the concept of financing, you've created a monster. You've taken someone who was mentally prepared to write the big check and started them thinking that they don't have to. Big mistake!

I have never once offered a customer financing. I have never even brought it up. When a customer asks me about it I say, "Sure, we'll only take a third down and we won't ask you for another dime until the job is done and you're happy with it."

I'd say that my closing ratio speaks for itself.

Lifetime Shingles

A lifetime is a very long time. Why do most people want a new roof? Most often, it's because their existing roof leaks or looks bad. When a customer asks me about the warranty on shingles, I tell them this:

"Have you ever looked at the miles per gallon listed on a new car's sticker? Do you believe that you can achieve that same result? Of course not. And it's no different with shingles. Shingle manufacturers have been playing around with their warranties a lot over the last several years. But you have to understand what a shingle warranty is. It's how long the manufacturer says that your shingles will hold together, without falling apart and letting water into your house, under perfect conditions. Is your new roof going to live its life under perfect conditions? Of course not. The manufacturers are not saying that is how long your new shingles will look good. If you doubt that, just try calling a manufacturer's rep and telling him you want to put in a warranty claim because your shingles look bad. After he finishes laughing, he'll explain that the warranty has nothing to do with the looks of the shingles. Most manufacturers determine the length of their warranty by testing the tensile strength of the matting on the bottom layer of the shingle—not the granules on top. But it's the granules on top that give the shingle color, texture, shadow, and look. It's the granules that make a shingle look good. A 50-year (or lifetime) warrantied shingle doesn't have any more granules on it, or very few more, than a 25 or 30-year shingle. So, it's not going to look good any longer. Usually, any roof, regardless of how many years its warranty, is only going to look good for 20 to 25 years ... if you're lucky. That's under perfect conditions. More often, you can expect them to look good for 16 to 18 years. Don't pick a shingle based on that. Pick the one that you like. If you have a special situation, like being high on a hill where your roof will catch a lot of wind, pick a heavier one. Otherwise, pick a pattern and color that you like, and forget the length of the warranty. It's going to be a moot point after 18 to 25 years anyway."

I have recited that to many manufacturer's reps over the years, and I've yet to have one dispute my reasoning. Enough said?

Sales Contests

Few things can motivate a roofing salesman like a good sales contest, especially if it has a nice reward for winning it. I've tried many different contests, and I've rarely seen one fail to inspire the team.

The best one is the standard Salesman of the Month, but it's important how you reward the winner. An individual plaque that the winner can take home and show his wife and hang on his wall is a no-brainer. But you should also have something displayed in the office to give the winner bragging rights, something that won't go away. I prefer the yearly plaque, with engraved plates for each month. Of course, there should be a monetary reward for winning as well. The individual plaque should be prepared quickly after the winner is determined, and presented at a sales meeting in front of the other guys.

I also like to take a picture of the winner holding his plaque, frame it, and display it on a wall in the front office, along with the pictures of previous months' winners.

If you have a parking lot that will allow it, you might have a good spot reserved for the current Salesman of the Month.

Of course, I didn't come up with any of these ideas. They've been used around sales forces for many years. But for some reason, most roofing companies don't use them. They'll start doing it, and then let it fade away after a month or two. Perhaps it's just too much trouble. Big mistake! I don't care if you are a small company with only one or two salesmen, come up with some way to reward your guys for achieving a particular number of sales, or dollar amount of gross sales. In that situation, I prefer some combination of number and amount, so that a guy doesn't win for selling one big job, or a lot of tiny ones.

Staff Bonuses/Incentives

Bonuses and incentives should not be paid only to salesmen. They should be paid to your office staff as well. Most owners, however, want to pay those bonuses based on the net profit of the company. I have been offered such incentive packages several times. I always turn them down, and I'm not shy about stating my reasons.

I never want to be put into a situation where I have to tell the owner of a company I don't think he should buy that new truck, or give so-and-so a raise, because it will affect the net profit of the company, and with it, my bonus.

Let's face it, owners of companies hide personal expenses in with company expenses all the time. I did when I was an owner, and I've never met an owner who didn't. But is it fair to reduce the bonus you pay to your production manager because you had a new fence installed around your swimming pool and hid that in the books as a company expenditure? Hell no!

Is it fair that the company pays the insurance on your wife's personal vehicle, effectively increasing your company's overhead and reducing the net profit of the company … and your sales manager's bonus? Hell no!

In short, base bonuses and incentives on gross profits, gross sales, or some other production guideline that won't be affected by you trying to save a little on your taxes. Otherwise, your managers will develop resentment every time you decide to purchase a new piece of equipment for the company, or hide a personal expenditure in with those of the company.

Happy Customer Bonuses

I've already discussed sales contests as great incentives for salesmen, and performance incentives for staff, but there is another way to reward them that is very effective. After each job is done, you should be mailing out a form to solicit feedback from your customers. The form should request feedback on the salesman, the crew, the office staff, and the job itself. You'll get more of them back if you include a self-addressed, stamped envelope.

When the feedback forms are received back at your office, someone should read them and determine whether the feedback was positive or negative. We like to put a big yellow smiley face on the positive ones, and a big red frown face on the negative ones. Copies of them should go into the salesmen's boxes. Copies of any negative ones should go in your box so that you can determine if there might be a way to correct the situation and turn the customer's opinion of the company into a positive one.

Bonus points can be given to salesmen and/or staff and/or crews when the feedback is positive, and deducted when the feedback is negative. You can have a nice prize for the monthly winners.

16

Business Tidbits

There are dozens of little tidbits that Deryl and I have picked up over the years. You probably already know most of them, but you may not, so I'll take a few minutes here to list and explain them.

The Problem With Accounting Software

QuickBooks, MS Money, Peachtree, and others, are great tools for accounting, but you should be very careful about making business decisions based on the reports they generate. We have used QuickBooks for our accounting software for years, and we love it. However, when it comes to evaluating our business, we turn to our Roofing Office Software instead of QuickBooks. Why? Because QuickBooks and the others are accounting software. They are designed to do accounting. And accountants live in their own little world that often bears little or no resemblance to reality.

QuickBooks shows that your sales are up at the end of January, but you don't know how that could be possible. Last January's weather was mild and business was great, but this January's weather made it impossible to work. How can QuickBooks show that this January is much better than last January? That's because QuickBooks doesn't count a sale until the work is done and the contract is paid in full. December was great and your guys made a lot of sales, and you got the jobs done, but you didn't get many of them collected until January. QuickBooks counts those as sales made in January. Last year, most of those great January sales weren't counted by QuickBooks until February or March.

QuickBooks shows that your overall percentage of profit on jobs is down. Your materials are a higher percentage of your gross sales, as is your labor. It would be very easy to conclude that your salesmen have been selling jobs at a lower percentage of profit than in the past. But, you've been monitoring the sales as they come in, and you've been very proud of your guys for selling at an even higher profit margin. And you've been monitoring the jobs as they've been completed. Again, your guys have been doing a great job. So how can QuickBooks show that your percentage of profit is down? Well, remember that batch of new designer railings you had installed at your house and stuck into a job's materials bills so that you could pass it off as a business expense? And do you remember a few months ago when you had those two workers help you dig the trenches for your new sprinkler system at your house, again sticking the labor onto a job so that you could count that as a business expense? Do you remember the other two or three dozen things you slipped into "business expense" in the same manner? All owners do it—at least all that I've ever known do. But they forget to consider the impact of those things when looking at a report generated by QuickBooks.

Also, if you have some unique way of calculating the commissions that you pay your salesmen, QuickBooks will probably be useless in helping you with that. It may provide you with all the information you need to do it, but your bookkeeper will still end up doing the calculations by hand.

QuickBooks says that your advertising expenditures have gotten way out of whack with your gross sales. Do you need to cut back on advertising? Maybe not. Maybe you are forgetting that you have to pay for your ADVO mail-outs in advance. You've already paid the huge bill, but the advertising hasn't gone out yet. Even then, it will take sixty to ninety days (perhaps longer) for the sales generated by the mail-out to show up in QuickBooks.

Deposit checks collected at the time of sale are liabilities in QuickBooks, not assets. They hurt your numbers because QuickBooks looks at a deposit check as a loan from the customer to you. Your liabilities went up drastically because you had a great selling month and your guys collected a lot of deposit checks from customers. (Yes, I know, the contract itself is an asset, so the deposit shouldn't have hurt your numbers, but it does in many of the reports you'll generate in QuickBooks.)

The bottom line is this: Use accounting software for accounting, please your CPA, to give him the numbers he needs to help you figure out how to pay less taxes. That's what accountants do (and that's also why I will never work for someone on a percentage of net profit basis). A CPA's job is to fiddle with the numbers to show less profit, thereby decreasing tax liability. QuickBooks is a great tool to help him do that.

A good lead and job tracking software will be much more useful to you when you are evaluating your day-to-day business. It will give you actionable intelligence about your jobs, production, advertising, crews, salesmen, and their productivity.

The Bull's Eye

It's on your back. Everyone is waiting for an opportunity to shoot at it. You're a contractor, and contractors have deep pockets—or so everyone seems to believe. People will sue you at the drop of a hat. You have to protect yourself. That's the nature of the business you're in, so deal with it.

In 2004, I was a member of Certainteed's Professional Roofers Advisory Council. We met at the Sheraton Hotel in Tyson's Corner, Virginia. There were about thirty of us present, mostly contractors, some supplier's representatives, and some manufacturer's representatives. We were there to discuss how to improve products and services at all phases of the business, so there were many topics covered.

Of the many hours that we were in that meeting, the topic that dominated the majority of the time was the recent lawsuits that had been filed against roofing companies (which the roofing companies almost always lost), and how to avoid becoming a victim of one.

Improper ventilation was the culprit. Mold and mildew and rotten wood had, according to the plaintiffs, resulted from the roofing contractors not installing proper ventilation at the time of their re-roof jobs. The roofing companies defended themselves by saying they offered to do it, but the customers didn't want to spend the extra money. That defense didn't fly, and the roofing companies lost.

, you must study proper ventilation techniques and
what you've learned. If a customer wants to trim a
estimate by chopping off the cost of proper ventila-
he job, or at least have them sign some kind of waiver
he possible result. That's what we've come to, so deal
with it.

Suppliers

A good supplier can be a great friend and ally. They can bail you out of jams, help you correct mistakes on short notice, and many other things. A bad supplier can be your worst nightmare.

I prefer picking one supplier and ordering 80 percent of my materials from them. Then, I pick a secondary supplier and give him the other 20 percent of my business. They should know about each other. Your secondary supplier should give you special treatment because he wants to become your primary supplier. Your primary supplier should give you great service to keep you from jumping ship and reversing the percentages.

Of course I look at price when picking a supplier. But, just as I tell my customers during a presentation, price is only one factor. I don't mind paying more for quality service. When I do compare prices, I don't let myself fall into the trap of looking only at the price of shingles. Suppliers play games with that a lot. They will charge you less for shingles, and then more than make up for it with higher prices on accessories.

I like to order everything for a job from the same place. So, to determine how different suppliers are charging, I take three or four jobs that I've done in the past, and see how much each supplier would have charged me for the entire material order. Most often, the prices of various items offset each other and the totals aren't much different.

Both my primary and my secondary supplier should be willing to stock some items just for me. No, I don't want them delivered to my office. That causes two problems: storage space and getting them to the job. I want my suppliers to inventory them for me, with the promise from me that I will use them.

I want one person at the supply company to handle all of my orders, not a different counter person every time. And I don't want that person to be my sales rep, who will be out in the field most of the time, not behind the counter. I want my counter person to personally handle every fax I send them. He'll know what he can substitute without calling to check with me first, and he'll catch mistakes on our orders. "Neal, I just got the fax on Job 4321 and there's no felt on it."

My suppliers won't charge me a restocking fee except in strange and unusual circumstances that I will agree to on a case-by-case basis. And, when I have leftover materials returned to them, they aren't (within reason) going to be too picky about the condition of the wrapper and such.

My suppliers will give me a discount on every bill for paying early, and I will take advantage of that. You can save thousands of dollars every year simply by paying your material bills early. To make that easier, I suggest paying them at least as often as weekly. Don't wait until the very last minute and then have to write a huge check. It's much more palatable to write several smaller ones.

Never send a payment to a supply company without a remittance sheet detailing exactly which invoices you are paying and how much discount you are taking on each one. I've seen owners fire off a check for $25,000 or $50,000 to a supply company just to "get them off his back." That never failed to cause problems later. We had no way to go back and figure out what invoices had been paid and which had not. Don't do that.

Manufacturer Rebates

Most manufacturers will give their good customers a rebate. Sometimes, they will agree to give you an x-amount rebate for each bundle of this, and y-amount for each bundle of that. Of course, they'll want you to keep up with that and provide copies of the invoices to document your numbers. I've done that and it's a pain in the ass. I prefer that the manufacturer keep up with it, whether it's the corporate office, or your local rep. One way or the other, you need to ask for (or demand, if you're a high volume company) rebates from your manufacturers.

With regard to those rebates, and discounts taken for paying your material bills early, don't feel guilty about not calculating them in when paying a salesman who is on a percentage of profit commission structure. The rebates and discounts are none of his business. They are administrative rewards paid to you by your suppliers and manufacturers. They are not part of the profit he generated on the job.

Credit Cards

We've become a "plastic" society. For a variety of reasons, including rewards and frequent flyer miles, almost everyone wants to pay for large ticket items, like a roof, on his credit card. You need to accept credit cards. It's a big hit on your profit though.

I don't like "punishing" customers, or salesmen, for a job being paid for by credit card. I don't like telling a customer, "If you want to pay by credit card, we have to add 3% to the price." I would much rather set my price higher and then tell the customer, "I'll give you a 3% discount if you pay by personal check." It just sounds better. Most often, however, when they pull out their checkbook, I don't offer the discount (if it never came up during the presentation and sale). The customer doesn't know that we've built the 3% into the price, so he doesn't know the difference. If you build the 3% into your price though, you won't be getting the full 3%. You'll still be paying commissions and taxes on the 3%, so keep that in mind when deciding how much to up the price.

Most credit card companies charge you a higher percentage if you "key in" the credit card number (especially if you don't have the proper billing address, which may be different than the job address). They charge you a lesser percentage if you "swipe" the credit card. There is less chance of fraud and disputed charges that way, so the credit card company is less at risk on those transactions.

It wouldn't be reasonable to ask a customer to drive to your office to have his card swiped, nor to give your salesman the card to go swipe and bring back later. The solution is hand-held, portable, battery-powered, credit card machines. I have one to use at expos and such when selling my

software. They cost a few hundred dollars, but they ⸝
even have an infrared printer that prints out receipts, (
for the customer to sign.

If you buy one of these machines through your credit card service, the,
will charge you a lot for them, perhaps double (or more) the amount
charged by the company that makes the machine. However, if you buy the
unit from the manufacturer, there may a problem with getting it pro-
grammed to suit your credit card service. I bought mine from the manufacturer and signed up to use their credit card service as well. That
simplified the whole matter, and they gave me just as good a rate as the
other credit card processing services (less than some). The company is
Electronic Data Payment Systems (and no, they don't pay me for saying
so, although maybe they should, heh-heh). The unit works through
AT&T Wireless. You don't have to have an account with AT&T, or a separate wireless account, it comes with the unit. And you're not charged for
minutes, or anything like that.

One of the beauties of using the machine is that it will tell you right
away if there is a problem with the credit card, whether it's declined or
whatever. I love my machine, and I suggest that you get one for each of
your salesmen (after they've been around awhile and have earned your
trust enough to hand them an expensive machine).

Beating The Insurance Auditor

Insurance Auditors do not have an easy job. Most companies, especially
roofing and construction companies, make them search through files and
records, check and cross check. It's a very time consuming effort. They are
always pressed for time. Their companies expect them to do too many
audits in a day.

Deryl has figured out how to make the whole process simple and pain-
less for them, and non-problematic for us. Usually they accept her numbers without questioning them. Here's how she does it:

Deryl does the audit for them. We do a fair job of keeping our subcon-
tractors' insurance certificates in order. And we know how much we've

aid each of them. Deryl gets everything ready and organized for the auditor, with printouts, copies of paperwork, and totals. She goes out of her way to highlight a sub or two that we've paid money to (small amounts that won't hurt us) who didn't have valid insurance. When auditors come in, they are always in a hurry to get finished and on to the next company, so when they see what she has ready for them their faces light up. They usually glance briefly (usually very briefly ... sometimes a little as 15 seconds) at her work, take their copies, thank her for being so organized, and leave. They don't dig around or question her numbers at all.

Taking the time to learn the audit process and how to prepare for an insurance audit is time well spent. And it will save you thousands of dollars in penalties.

Your Cell Phone Service and Rep

Okay, now I'm touching on a topic that will probably make the hair on the back of your neck stand up. Straightening out a problem with a cell phone bill can be one of the most frustrating, most irritating, most aggravating experiences you'll ever have. NVR has over 25 cell phones to deal with, so we've had a lot of dealings with the likes of Nextel. Aaaarrrrgggg!!!

Here's what we've learned: First and foremost, never go though an independent service or rep to get your cell phone service. Go straight to the source, and get them to assign a rep to handle your account.

Independent reps and services can toss a great sales pitch about "We'll be right there to straighten out any problems." Bullshit! We've even had Nextel say about the plan we signed up for (several months after signing up for it), "No, we don't have any plan like that. I don't know where your rep came up with that, but we're not going to honor it." That battle raged on for over a year. Our rep stalled and beat around the bush until we gave him the boot and started dealing straight with Nextel. Even then, it took several more months to get everything straightened out.

Going through an independent third party is rarely wise, regardless of what you're signing up for, but going that route on your cell phone service is just asking for trouble.

When you hand an employee a company cell phone, make sure you explain that any text messaging, GPS, web access, or other similar charges will be charged to him/her. Even then, it's an accounting nightmare, so take them out behind the woodshed if they use those kinds of services on your company cell phone.

You And Your Banker

If your bank rep is not on your Christmas card list, you obviously don't get it.

Your staff screwed up, or the bank did. Either way, you don't have enough in your account to cover some of the checks that came to the bank that day. What would you like to see happen? I would like to know that my bank rep says, "Don't bounce those checks just yet. There's obviously a mistake somewhere. I'll give Neal or Deryl a call and ask them what's going on."

Or, you're out of town and one of your people needs to cash a check, or write one to a business where you don't have an account. You're not there to sign it. You call the bank and tell your rep, "I'm going to have Karen write a check and sign my name 'by her'. Please make sure there isn't a problem when it hits the bank."

> McLean, Texas, 1979. A hitchhiker came down Route 66 (dozens a day passed by our restaurant). He was a teenager and had his young wife with him. I put them both to work, gave them a place to sleep, and gave them something to eat. Two days later, the kid came to me and asked to borrow $300 to buy Hembright's old station wagon. I told him that I might consider it after he'd been there for two or three weeks, but I didn't know him well enough yet. ($300 was a lot of money in 1979.) He and his wife didn't show up for work the next day, and I never saw them again.
>
> Several months later, I got a call from Jim Allison, the president of the bank, asking me how I wanted to handle the car loan that was in default at the bank. I didn't know what he was talking about, so I headed down to the bank to see Jim.

When I was sitting in Jim's office, he began telling me about the kid who came in and said that I'd sent him. "He told me that you said you'd co-sign on the $300 note for him to buy Hembright's station wagon, so I gave him the money."

I related to Jim that the boy had come to me first and I'd refused to give him the money, and that I hadn't sent him to the bank or agreed to co-sign on a loan for him. Jim got red in the face and said, "Oh well, my mistake. I should have called you to confirm the kid's story." I agreed and left, still shaking my head.

That evening, I was sitting in my dad's porch swing, helping him polish off a half gallon bottle of Jim Beam. I told him about the whole deal with the kid and the car and the bank. My dad got very serious. "Son, you know what you've got to do, don't you?" I didn't, so I shook my head. "Tomorrow morning, you go to the restaurant and get $150 out of the safe, and go give it to Jim."

I was stunned and I said so. "It wasn't my fault. Jim screwed up. Why should I pay anything?"

"Neal, how much is your good name and reputation worth in this town? Is it worth $150? Your banker just gave a kid a $300 loan … just for mentioning your name. I'd say that's a reputation worth forking over $150 to protect, wouldn't you?"

The next day, I did as my father had "suggested." When I handed Jim the envelope and he peeked inside it, he grinned up at me. "You didn't happen to mention anything about this whole car thing to your dad last night, did you?" When I said that I had, he grinned even wider and said, "Your dad's a very smart man."

Get to know your bank rep. Don't always send someone else to the bank for you. Go there sometimes—and go inside, not through the drive-up. Take a few minutes to sit and visit with your rep, even when you don't have any business to do with them. You don't want them thinking that you only care about them when you need something. Develop a relationship with them … and a reputation.

The Games They Play

Employees can come up with some very imaginative ways to screw you over. I don't like to think in those terms, but it's a fact of life. I would rather always think positively about my people, but I believe what Ronald Reagan said is the best policy: "Trust but verify."

If your salesmen know that you won't accept a job under x percentage of gross profit, and they have a big deal that falls below that, they may be tempted to play with the numbers to get it to show the profit above your minimum.

It's very difficult to distinguish between that and other times when they just make a mistake. The easiest way to catch it is to have your staff print out a copy of every job that caps out under your minimum after all the bills have come in on it, and put it in your box for review. A salesman who has too many jobs show up in your box is either playing games, or he is making too many mistakes. Either way, you need to deal with it.

A homeowner calls the office and has some complaint about his job, but your staff can't find any record of the job. Upon investigating further, you find that the salesman, or a crew member, did some work on the side for extra cash. Regardless of whether it was for a customer you sent them to, or the neighbor of a customer you sent them to, the customer had the idea that they were dealing with your company, not an individual. And either way, it's stealing. This is not a "three strikes and you're out" deal, it's stealing and it is grounds for immediate termination. Even if the salesman or crew member didn't realize that he was doing something egregiously wrong, fire him anyway. He's either pulling your leg, or he doesn't have enough moral and ethical sense to realize stealing when he sees it. Sometimes it will involve a salesman and a crewman working together. Fire them both. The crewman will probably feign innocence, saying he didn't know what the salesman was doing, that he didn't know it was an under the table deal. Fire him anyway. He should know better than to do work without a company work order, and he knows that the company doesn't give a salesman cash to give to a crew for work. He knew, and if he didn't, gross stupidity is an offence worthy of termination too.

There is an acceptable way they can do that work on the side. "Neal, the homeowner wants this done. I can do that kind of work, and I could use the extra money. Can I do it?"

"Well, we don't want that kind of job anyway, so you can do it on these conditions. First, you must wait until all of our work for that customer (or his neighbor, whichever the case may be) has been completed and paid in full. Then, you have to make it very clear to the customer that our company isn't involved, that it's between you and them. And lastly, only if I call them and verify that they have a full and complete understanding that we're not involved and that they shouldn't call us if they have problems with the job you do for them."

The phones are busy and one of your salesmen is in the office. He helps out the staff by fielding some calls. If he takes a lead, it must be processed and handed out just like any other lead. If it's a really nice deal and he pockets it, that's stealing. However, if he brings it to you and explains that he really hit it off with the customer, and he'd like to run it, it's your call. I like to reward guys for helping out with the phones when things get crazy, so sometimes I toss them a bone like that as a reward. Be careful though. You don't want to create an "office hawk" that will spend a lot of time answering the phones so that he can swoop down and sink his claws into a good lead.

A really smart salesman (or at least a really devious one) might be imaginative enough to slide a staff member a few bucks under the table for a really nice lead, and perhaps a few bucks more if he closes it. Usually, warning your staff that you'll fire them for accepting such a bribe is enough to dissuade them from doing it. I don't warn the salesmen not to try it though. I don't want to give them any ideas that they haven't thought of on their own. Fire the staff member that you catch accepting a bribe for good leads. You can't afford for your salesmen to get the idea that your office is a "survival of the most corrupt" kind of place (like Congress).

I don't agree with everything John Francis does, but one thing I've seen him do really impressed me. When he caught someone stealing, regardless of how, he called a meeting of everyone in the company. And then he fired the person right there in front of everyone. That struck me as being wrong at first, but the more I thought about it, the more sense it made to me. It's one thing for everyone to hear that someone got fired for stealing, but it's another thing to see it happen. No one who has seen it would like to be in the position of the one getting fired right in front of everyone else in the company. I know it made an impression on me, and I could tell by the faces of the others in the room that it made an impression on them too. (The only time he did this was when the person was getting fired for stealing, not for other things.)

You give a salesman or crew member a company credit card to use for something specific. They use it for something else. "But I was hungry and I didn't have any money on me. I was going to tell Deryl to take it out of my next check. I wasn't trying to steal from you, honest." Bullshit! I keep my cell phone with me 24–7. He could have called me. I may let him off with a warning once, but not twice.

A referral lead wound up in the wrong hands. The wrong salesman got it. It happens ... sometimes too often. When it does, it's almost always on a nice deal, not a little doghouse. You and your staff should go to great lengths to prevent it from happening, but it will sometimes happen anyway. The customer didn't ask for the salesman by name, or it was just a crazy day in the office and the staff member who took the call let it slip through the cracks.

When a salesman comes to me with a complaint about his referral ending up in someone else's hands, I always tell him the same thing, "Hey, it happens. I'll look into it and see if I can find out how it happened. I'll get back to you on it." And then I do everything I can to find out how it happened. Most often, it was an honest mistake, so I'll call in the salesman who got the lead by mistake, explain the problem, and strongly suggest that he split the commission with the other salesman. "However, he shouldn't get a free ride. You've done a lot of work on this deal. He should earn his half. Make him babysit the job and help you with any problems. Make him stay involved." Then, I have that same conversation with the salesman who should have gotten the lead in the first place.

Appleton, Wisconsin, 1998. I was babysitting one of my jobs in progress. A neighbor came over and began talking to me. He liked the way we were handling things for his neighbor. He wanted estimates on his house and his six rental houses. I did all seven estimates for the guy the next day. It took me all day. Deryl wasn't in the truck with me that week. One of the girls in the office needed some time off, so Deryl was helping out in the office.

A few days later, Burk, one of the other salesmen, jumped all over me (verbally) about stealing his lead. "That was a referral from one of my customers, but when I got out there, you'd already been there. It was seven houses, nice ones. I should have known that none of the rest of us had a chance with your wife working in the office."

I talked until I was blue in the face, trying to convince Burk that Deryl hadn't given me the lead, but he didn't believe me. Actually, I wasn't taking any leads from the office then. I didn't need them, but Burk wouldn't buy that. Finally, I told him, "Look, obviously you need the jobs more than I do, so come on out to my truck and I'll give you my copies of the estimates. You can have them. They're not worth all this shit to me." And that's what I did.

I had the last laugh though. That guy ran Burk around in circles for weeks, dealing with his insurance company, negotiating with them and arguing with them. Finally, when the guy got the insurance checks, he pocketed the money and told Burk to take a long walk off of a short pier. When Burk told me about it later, all I could say was, "Be careful what you ask for."

When a situation comes up that requires two salesmen to split a commission, I don't want the office handling the split. I want there to be one salesman responsible for the job. I'll pay that salesman, and it's up to him to pay the other salesman. I warn him about income taxes on the money though. He shouldn't split the commission right down the middle. He should take enough extra to cover his taxes on the whole thing.

Your Crews

I have lectured owners, salesmen, and office staff about how important it is to develop meaningful relationships with their crews. After all, without them we can all go flip hamburgers for a living. Deryl and I don't just pay lip service to that. We are serious about it.

Deryl's Babies

When we opened our own company in Oshkosh, Wisconsin in early 2000, I was fortunate to get a couple of crews to come work for me that I'd worked with in years past. The minute I said, "Deryl and I are starting our own company," they said, "We're on our way. Where are you?" We didn't know all of their men, but we knew the foremen. We made it a point to get to know all of them, but the language difference sometimes made it difficult.

Still, we would go eat at their favorite "real Mexican food" restaurants with them, and we took all of them, and their wives and kids, on a party boat down the Fox River. A couple of them spoke enough English to translate for us, so we had great conversations with all the guys and their wives. There were fireworks displays in the park, birthday parties ... we became friends.

One night, there was a frantic pounding on our door. It was 3 a.m. When we got to the door, we saw the excited face of one of the crewmen. "Baby comes ... you come hospital." He practically begged Deryl.

Deryl threw on some clothes and went with him. I didn't see her again until late the next day. It had been a difficult labor, and Deryl was exhausted. Later, she told me about how the doctors and nurses had reacted to her being there.

"Does she work for you?"

"No, we're just friends," Deryl answered.

"But you don't speak Spanish, and she doesn't speak English."

"We're still friends. We get by."

Of course, the doctors and nurses didn't know what to say to that. Obviously, the crewman and his wife didn't trust the people at the hospital, especially since no one there spoke Spanish, but they trusted Deryl to look after their best interests.

Two months later, another frantic knock on our door at 2 a.m. (Why do women always go into labor in the middle of the night?) The doctors and nurses didn't question Deryl's presence this time. They didn't understand it, but they accepted it.

And so it went. The months passed, the frantic knocks on the door continued, and our family grew. When Deryl and I left Wisconsin, the crews didn't come with us. They had settled in and made that their home. We still get calls from them though, or at least the one that speaks the best English, updating us on the status of all the families ... and any new additions to them.

Never forget that your roofers are people, worthy of your respect, your trust, your loyalty, and your friendship. There is no such thing as a language barrier. There are only language hurdles, and they aren't tall ones.

Leftovers

I have heard salesmen, managers, owners, and even homeowners complain for years about crews throwing full bundles of shingles into the trash. I know it happens sometimes, and I know why, just as you do. I have a way of cutting down on how much of that goes on.

Crews are accustomed to getting paid for the number of squares of shingles they install. If you send out twenty squares, and there are two squares left over, most companies will pay the crew for eighteen squares. That is the first of two situations that causes the problem. The second problem is that many companies require the crew to return leftover materials to the office. When combined, we are asking a crew to do more work for less pay. Hmm, how keen would you be on that idea, if you were in their shoes? I'm guessing not very.

I let my crews know that I'm going to pay them for the number of squares delivered, regardless of whether they install all of them or not. There are exceptions though. If the salesman really screwed up and sent thirty squares to do a fifteen square house, obviously we're not going to pay them for thirty squares. We have to be reasonable. But, if there are two or three squares of shingles left over, I do not deduct that from their pay. And my salesmen are required to return the leftover shingles to the office or supply company, so I'm not asking the crew to do more work. So, I get my leftover shingles back; they have no incentive for throwing them away. If the salesman ordered too few shingles and we had to go get more, the crew will be paid for the additional shingles.

Oh, I know what you're thinking. If there are leftover shingles, the customer might say, "Hey, I paid for those. I want them." Or they might say, "You need to lower my price because you charged me for too many squares." So you want to get those leftovers out of there before the customer sees them.

Any salesman or manager who can't handle that situation should find other employment. I've handled it dozens of times as a salesman, and many more times as a manager. And it's never caused a happy customer to be unhappy as a result (that I know of). It's not difficult. "Sir, we always try to send out more materials than we think we're going to need. Having a few too many on the job is a lot better than being a bundle short, especially since we probably won't know it until after the supply house is already closed."

"I paid for those shingles."

"No sir, actually you paid for exactly enough materials to do your job, no more, no less. If I had measured wrong and had to go get another bundle, or ten, you wouldn't take kindly to being asked for more money. You'd tell me that you paid to have your roof done, not a specific number of squares. Nowhere in our estimate or on our contract does it specify how many shingles we're charging you for. You're being charged for exactly what it takes to do the job, no more, no less."

If there are a few bundles left over, I always ask the customer if he'd like to have one or two to store in his garage for repairs later. I warn him though, that after a couple of years, the shingles on the roof and the shingles in his garage won't match (because of fading).

And now for the larger issue … money. Owners are always quick to want to save a few dollars here and there, and leftover shingles given away or thrown away eats on them. Hey, I can understand that, but I still tell them to put it out of their minds and get over it. Actually, those leftover shingles, even if thrown in the trash, made them money. You are charging the customer based on a percentage over and above the cost of the materials and labor. If the salesman ordered too many shingles, the contract price was higher, and you made profit on the higher dollar amount. The same holds true for the labor.

You should set your profit percentage at an amount that you can be happy with, then live with the results. Don't wear yourself, your salesmen, or your crews out by trying to save a dollar or 20 over and above the profit percentage that you would have been happy with anyway. Save all of that stress and concern for more important matters.

Summary

I would boil down my formula for success this way:

1. Develop your vision and then commit to it … really commit to it.

2. Surround yourself with good people. Talent is second to dedication.

3. Install "systems" for your office and cross train your staff.

4. Develop a solid roofing philosophy. Install the best roofing system possible.

5. Hire a professional sales force. Strength of character comes before talent.

6. Train them thoroughly, getting to know them in the process, and they you.

7. Equip them properly. You want them to feel like professionals from the first day.

8. Check on their performance. Hold them accountable. Keep training them.

9. Cull the bad, the negative, the disbelievers, the non-committed, and the slackers.

10. Learn to love your people: staff, salesmen, and crews—really love them.

11. Do right by your customers. Walk the walk. Don't just pay it lip service.

12. Go fishing sometimes, and don't bait your hook. Just sit back and relax, clear your head, and refocus on the vision. Renew your commitment to building your company by building your reputation.

13. Don't get impatient. Don't give up. Don't quit. It takes time.

So there you have it. I could probably go on for another two hundred pages or so, but I think you should have the idea by now. You must develop a clear vision of what you want to achieve and then inspire others to want to achieve it too. **The goal, however, must be worthy of inspiration.**

> *If a man is called to be a street sweeper, he should sweep streets even as Michelangelo painted, or Beethoven composed music, or Shakespeare wrote poetry. He should sweep streets so well that all the hosts of heaven and earth will pause to say, here lived a great street sweeper who did his job well."*
>
> —*Martin Luther King, Jr.*

A personal note from Neal and Deryl:

One last thought before we send you off to read our stories (and we hope that you do). From our hearts Deryl and I would like to thank you for giving us this opportunity to share our thoughts, our ideas, our feelings, and our experiences with you. May the god of success shine his light on you … but only if you are, or you strive to be, a good person.

—Neal and Deryl Middleton

"To find out what kind of leader you are, turn around and look at who is following you."

Now, go build yourself a company that you can be proud of.

My Stories

I have hundreds of stories of my experiences in the roofing business. I have related many of them to you in the previous chapters when I felt they weren't too long, and when I felt they were pertinent to the topic. I have many more, but they're not just stories. There is a point to each and every one of them. I typically relate most of them to my trainees, not to bore them or to entertain them, but to teach them. If they survive in the roofing business, they will run across many of these situations. When they do, I don't want them to panic, or become frustrated, or be overwhelmed by the experience. I want them to be able to say: "This is almost like that thing that happened to Neal, so it's not that big of a deal." Or, one of my stories may help them avoid making the same mistake I've made in the past, or perhaps inspire them, or motivate them, or simply make them laugh. If my stories accomplish any one of those things, then they are worth telling.

The Rocket Scientist

Indianapolis, Indiana, 2002. We hired a man who had previously been working for NASA in Houston. I don't think I ever knew what kind of work he did for NASA, but we just called him our rocket scientist.

One day, while a group of us—the owner of the company, his son, several salesmen, my wife and I—were having lunch at Chili's, my phone rang. It was the rocket scientist and he was in a total panic. "Neal, I screwed up big time. I only ordered half enough shingles on this job. I don't know what I'm going to do."

I had seen the house, and I could vaguely remember the material order, so I didn't understand how he could be that short of shingles. When I asked him, and he explained the problem, I sat there speechless for several seconds. I didn't know what to say.

Finally, I told him that I was in Chili's and that I was having trouble hearing him, could he please repeat what he'd said. At the same time, I was waving my hand for everyone at our table to be quiet. He repeated what he had said, and I still couldn't believe what I was hearing.

I asked him to repeat it for a third time, but this time I hit the speaker button on my phone and set it in the center of the table, urging everyone to listen. They all leaned in to hear over the other noise in the restaurant.

"I said: I screwed up big time. I only ordered half enough shingles. There are two layers on the house and I only ordered enough to put one layer of new shingles back on it."

Everyone else at the table reacted about as I had. They were stunned. Brent, the owner's son, and manager of the company, was the one who had trained the guy. His face became bright red and he quickly grabbed the phone, took it off speaker, and said, "This is Brent. Tell me what the problem is again." As he was listening, he got up and walked outside, so we couldn't hear what he was telling the salesman. The rest of us had gotten over our shock enough to burst out in laughter, when Deryl asked, "Isn't he the rocket scientist?"

Never take anything for granted when training a new salesman—not even if he's a rocket scientist.

Validation

I can't imagine not telling you about the most wonderful, the most satisfying, the most joyful phone conversation I've ever had in my life.

I've had plenty of bad ones.

My sister called me from the hospital an hour after I'd left there. "Neal, you'd better get back up here. The doctor wants to talk to us and it doesn't look good." When I arrived, the doctor explained that my mother was brain dead and that we needed to make a decision about pulling the plug.

Thirty-six hours later, my sister called again, this time from her home 350 miles away. "Neal, it's dad. He died in his sleep."

Several years later, my niece called the night before I was to have 13 tumors removed from my intestines. "Neal, it's Mom. When I got home from work, she was unconscious. She died at the hospital a few minutes ago."

I've had those kinds of phone calls, but I had one which overshadowed every one of them and made up for them, one which validated me as a worthwhile and productive member of the marriage partnership.

Indianapolis, Indiana, June 1996. The company was giving me a $250 draw every week. It was barely enough for gas and food. To get money to Deryl to help pay the bills, we had set up a bank account in Indiana. Her name was on the signature card, so she could write checks on the account. I would deposit my draw checks, less what I needed to make it through the week, and I would call her every Friday to tell her how much she could transfer into our Texas account to help pay the bills.

It was the same conversation every Friday. "You can have $25 or $50 max, but no more. I need money for gas and food. I'm doing good, but I'm just not there yet. I'll make it up to you. I promise."

"Neal, we're getting behind on the bills. You're not making any money, so why don't you come home and get a real job? We can't make it like this."

And then, one Thursday, I had a flat tire while going up the I-465 loop around Indianapolis. When I lowered my spare from under the bed of my S-10, I found that it had a gash in it. Evidently something had been thrown up from the road and torn it wide open. I had less than $10 in my pocket.

I didn't know what else to do, so I walked the mile to the nearest pay phone and paged Bobby Powers. (We didn't have cell phones back then.) He returned my call a few minutes later and told me not to worry, that he was on his way. So I walked back to my truck and waited for him to make the 45-minute drive from the other side of Indianapolis.

When Bobby arrived, he took me to Wal-Mart and bought me a tire. On the way back to my truck, I told him, "Bobby, I can't do this anymore. I'm tired of being broke. I think I'm doing okay. I'm making some sales, but I just can't live like this. The pressure from home is mounting. I'm afraid that I'm going to have to call it quits and go back to Texas."

Bobby knew what I was feeling. "You need to talk to Marty. I can do it for you, but sooner or later, you're going to have to start sticking up for yourself. Go talk to Marty in the morning and tell him that you need more money."

The next day, I was in Marty's office, determined to get more money or quit. Marty stared at me hard. Then he flopped open his checkbook and asked, "How much do you need?"

"Five hundred a week," I said in a tone that I hoped would sound more confident than I felt.

Marty reared back his head in feigned shock, and then he smiled and winked at me. "Why don't we just settle up then? You've been doing pretty good. We'll settle up now, and then I'll start paying you every week on the collections you bring in. All we have to do is figure up how much you've earned so far, and deduct what I've paid you, and I'll write you a check for the difference."

So that's what we did. Quite honestly, I didn't even know what my commission was supposed to be until he explained it to me that day. All I knew was that Bobby had said I could make a lot of money, and I trusted him. He was my friend. Marty explained that my commissions were to be 10% of my collections.

Later that evening, I called Deryl. "How much can I write a check for this week?" she asked.

"I don't know. How much do you need?"

"Neal, we're getting way behind on the bills. I need some money. This just isn't working. You need to come home and get a real job. I mean it. It's getting serious."

I was doing a great job of containing my laughter. "Deryl, why don't you write a check for five?"

"Five! You're kidding. I'm serious. I need money for the bills. Five dollars won't buy dog food."

"I didn't mean five dollars. I was thinking of a little more than that."

"You don't mean five hundred? Damnit Neal, I'm serious. How much can I write a check for?"

I took a deep breath and then let it out slowly. "Deryl, I was thinking more like five thousand."

She went ballistic. "Damnit, Neal! Don't do this to me. Quit playing around. I'm serious. Things are getting really bad. We need some money. Now, how much can I write a check for this week?"

"Deryl, I'm not bullshitting. If you write a check for five thousand dollars, it will clear my bank here. I'm not kidding. I'm as serious as a heart attack."

"You're serious?"

"Yes, I'm serious. I want you to transfer five thousand dollars from my bank here into your account there. It will clear my bank. I promise. Use it to catch up on the bills, go shopping, or whatever you want."

There was a long silence before Deryl asked in a very serious tone, "Neal, are you doing something illegal?"

I can't describe to you how I felt at that moment. I had been vindicated. All of my failed schemes to make money had been erased in one fell swoop. I was no longer a "dreamer," no longer a "wishful thinker," no longer "too gullible" or too "naïve." I was no longer a failure, not in her eyes, and not in mine. I had been validated.

The following Friday, I told Deryl to transfer $3,500 from my account, and the week after that $2,500 and the week after that $4,500, and on and on and on. She couldn't believe it. I couldn't believe it. We were both floating on the clouds. The bills were paid up. We had extra money in our checking account. We were just embarking on the trip that is the American dream.

I'm happy to report to you that we've never failed to look back. In fact, we look back all the time. When we do, we have to pinch ourselves to insure that we're not dreaming. We may be living the dream, but that wouldn't mean very much if we didn't keep constantly reminding ourselves of what it was like before I got into the roofing business. We especially like to muse over that when we're lying side by side in hammocks stretched between palm trees on some Caribbean island, or pausing before starting down the next slope of our favorite ski resort.

The Sun Bather

Virginia Beach, Virginia, 1997. I was on a three-story apartment building with a 3–12 straight gable roof, two blocks from the beach, on a beautiful summer day. The roof was no problem to walk on or measure. In fact, it was rather boring—that is, until I happened to glance down and ahead into the backyard of the house next door.

The lady's maker had … blessed her, and she was sunning face up in a state intended to avoid tan lines … any tan lines. She was wearing sunglasses, and nothing else. I decided my measurement of the length would be more accurate if taken from near the eave on that side of the roof. It was a hundred feet long—exactly a hundred feet long—thankfully.

I hooked my ball over the rake edge and began walking toward the other end … and her. When I had traversed 75 feet, I was right over her … and I was a tad distracted by the view. In fact, I didn't glance forward again until my 100-foot tape hit the end.

The toes of my right foot were hanging over the rake edge, and my left foot was suspended in midair, over nothing. Had the roof been one step shorter, I would have gone right over the edge and down three stories. I couldn't catch my balance enough to get my left foot back under me and onto the roof.

In the seconds that followed, I evaluated the possible courses of action available to me. There was a school bus below, but it was too far out. I didn't think I could push off enough to land on it. After all, my toes weren't even on the roof.

I was twirling my arms, frantically trying to regain my balance. Luckily, the ball on the end of my tape was hooked firmly on the opposite rake edge, and since the tape was at its maximum length, it provided me with a modicum of connection to the roof. As my hand went forward, the tension of the tape was just enough to pull me back. I got my left foot down and took a step backward.

I sat in my truck for half an hour before my hand stopped shaking enough to write down the measurements and use my calculator. I doubt that the lady even noticed that I almost died from looking at her. It's true, looks can kill.

What Was He Thinking?

Mooresville, Indiana, 1996. It was my first year in the roofing business. Mooresville is a small town (population around 5,000) a few miles south of Indianapolis. We'd been in town a couple of months and we were really starting to rock and roll.

Bobby Powers got a phone call from one of his customers whose roof was being done that day. "We've got a serious problem. The police are here. One of your crew guys … maybe you'd better just get over here and find out for yourself."

Bobby had been in the business awhile, so he'd seen and heard just about everything … or so he thought. A member of his roofing crew had broken into the house next-door to where they were doing the job. When that homeowner got home and went upstairs, he found our roofer in his bedroom, totally naked, standing on his bed … masturbating.

Word spread through our company within minutes, even before the police drove off with our roofer. We just knew that in a town like Mooresville, word of the incident would make its way to everyone in town by the next day. We would be finished. No one would want to hire us to do their roof—not after hearing about "the incident."

Actually though, nothing of the sort happened. Why? Oddly enough, it was the owner of the home the roofer broke into who saved us. The story he told everyone was: "You can't blame that poor boy. I'd been watching the crew work next door all day. It was hot—too hot for them to be up on that roof all day like that. The poor boy must have gotten heat stroke. You can't blame him. He obviously was delirious and didn't know what he was doing."

Uh, yeah, okay, I'll buy that. Whatever works, heh-heh-heh.

And the moral of the story … when you think you've seen it all, you haven't.

Precious Tulips

Indiana, 1997. The lady's house was large, with a long front slope to the 12–12 pitched roof. Her flowerbed was on the opposite end of the house from the driveway and in it there were four rows of beautiful tulips in full bloom.

I looked at the pitch of the roof and then at the position of the flowerbed and told her, "I'm sorry to have to tell you this, but your flowers are probably not going to survive the roofing job. Your roof is steep, and we lose a lot of control. Anything that slides off will probably land right in your flowerbed. We'll do what we can to protect them, but you might as well prepare yourself mentally for them to be destroyed." She looked sad, but she understood.

When the crew showed up to do the job, I admonished the foreman to do everything he could to protect those flowers, but I held out little hope that he would be successful. When I returned late that evening, the job was almost finished, and the flowers were still standing proudly … every one of them. In fact, the crew was totally finished working on that end of the house. All they lacked was installing a few ridge caps on the opposite (driveway) end, 60 or more feet away from the flowerbed.

The customer came outside, and we stood together in front of the flowerbed, admiring her beautiful tulips and sharing our relief that they had survived. One of the crewmen was on the opposite end of the house, cutting ridge caps and sailing the scrap triangular pieces down and into the back of the truck. The breeze caught one of them just right and carried it toward the flowerbed. We were both staring at the flowers, so we never saw it coming. All we saw was the clip, clip, clip as the piece of shingle sliced the tops off of three tulips as cleanly as if they had been cut by a master gardener.

The lady looked at me with a tear running down her face, shrugged and said with a sigh, "Well, at least we only lost three of them."

Delicate things sometimes do not survive a construction project. Prepare your customer for the worst and then hope for the best.

The Non-Believers

Omaha, Nebraska, 2001. I was in the process of closing up my Oshkosh, Wisconsin office and my Chicago office, and I was betting that Omaha was the storm that would make me some good money. It was a good storm, even though the insurance companies weren't paying the kind of money we were used to receiving in the union labor states.

I'd hired a General Manager to run that office for me, because I was still spending much of my time going back and forth from Oshkosh to Chicago to Omaha. Having three offices in three different states is a bitch, to say the least. My Omaha GM's name was Britt Moreland. I'd sold roofs alongside him in Virginia Beach and I knew that he'd later sold for Marty in Denver. I knew he could sell roofs, but the jury was still out on his management ability.

Several months into the storm, and many, many thousands of dollars into my bank account, I began getting frustrated. His salesmen just weren't producing, but I didn't know why. I hadn't trained them, and I didn't really even know them. He'd hired them and trained them right there in Omaha.

Finally, I couldn't take it anymore, so I told Britt to call a sales meeting. "I want every employee of the company there. If they don't show up, they're fired. I won't care what their excuse is."

Britt asked me, "What are you going to say to them?"

"I don't know, but it won't be a dull meeting. I can promise you that."

It was 7 pm on the last day of the month. The salesmen were all present, sitting on the opposite side of the folding table from me. DeAmber, our receptionist, was there, as was Deryl, my wife. There was a wall behind me with a whiteboard on it. I could tell by their body language that the employees had no idea what to expect. They didn't know me. They only knew that I was the owner and that my wife signed their checks. I was the mysterious guy that spent his time in the room upstairs in the cubby-hole of a corporate office. But of course, I believed in the chain of command, so I had purposely not interacted with them too much. They reported to Britt. He reported to me. Like I said … they didn't know me.

"Your sales totals are shit! That's going to change, and it's going to change right now. I don't know you, so I don't know what it's going to take to motivate you. But I can tell you this: if things don't change in a hurry, I'm going to close this office down and go play some golf. Golf is cheaper than supporting an unproductive office."

They all looked like deer caught in the headlights. They didn't know how to react, so they just sat there and stared at me with blank expressions. "We're going to have a sales contest … one like you've never seen before. I'm going to give the winner two thousand dollars. How does that sound?" They all perked up, so I continued, turning to the whiteboard and writing as I talked. "You have to make twenty sales in the next calendar month to qualify. Anyone who makes twenty sales will get one thousand dollars, and the winner will get two thousand. A sale has to be at least three grand to count, and those over seven grand will count as two sales. Any questions?"

When I was finished writing on the whiteboard, I turned to them and saw them rolling their eyes. Their expressions and body language told me that they didn't think that making twenty sales in a month was possible. I was speechless, but not for long. "You guys don't believe that it's possible to make twenty sales in a month, do you?" They all shook their heads, every single one of them. I was flabbergasted.

Finally, I issued them a challenge. "I'll tell you what then, I'll give you a choice. I'll let you decide whether you want to accept the terms of the sales contest as I've outlined them, or, if you don't think it's possible to qualify, I'll go out and try it myself. I'll be starting cold. I don't have anything in my pipeline. I won't take any leads from the office. If that's the way you want to play it, I'll go out and try to make some sales for the next month. Whatever I make in total sales is what the minimum will be to qualify for the two grand. It's your call. I want you to vote on which way to go." Then I turned to Britt and said, "I'll be outside having a cigarette. Come get me when the voting is over."

Ten minutes later, Britt eased up along side me. I was leaning against the tailgate of my truck with my foot up on the bumper. "Well, it looks like you're going to be out in the field selling for the next month," he said.

I shrugged and said in a somber tone, "They don't get it, do they, not a single f—ing one of them?"

He shook his head. "No, they don't. I've tried my best, but I haven't been able to get through to them. Maybe you can. I hope so." And then he laughed and added, "Those guys are in for one hell of a surprise."

I nodded. "Yep, they're about to meet Neal Middleton the salesman. I don't know if they'll survive it, but at this point, I don't really give a shit."

Britt laughed again. "I can't wait to see this."

After I snuffed out my cigarette, I strode back inside with Britt tagging along like an expectant father following the doctor down the hall to the delivery room. When I got inside, Deryl was leaning on the front counter grinning. DeAmber was behind her desk, anxious to see how it would all play out. She was a young black girl, a single mother with two grade-school-age kids. She lived with her mother, so she had a built-in babysitter. Girls like that are always looking for ways to pick up a little extra money.

I stood in front of our salesmen and said, "Okay, you non-believers are about to see a real roofing salesman in action." Then I turned to DeAmber and asked her, "Girl, how would you like to make some extra money?" She answered, "Hell yeah!" so I said, "I want you in here for two hours every weekday evening for the next two weeks. You're going to do some telemarketing for me. I'll pay you ten bucks an hour, plus ten bucks for every lead you get me. How does that sound?"

After DeAmber agreed, one of the salesmen said, "That's not fair. We don't have that kind of money to toss around."

I stared at him hard. "How many times have you had your lazy ass in Britt's office over the last three months, begging for money to pay your rent, or fix your truck, or money for gas … three, four, or was it five times? Have we ever said no to you? Have we ever refused to give you money … f—no! What makes you think that if you came in asking for money to use to generate leads for yourself, we'd say no? You're just too f—ing lazy to come up with an idea on your own. You'd rather whine and complain and bitch that the office isn't feeding you enough leads. You all know that DeAmber is a single mother, struggling to get by. But not a G—D—one of you thought of how to use her situation to improve your business. Now, when I leave here in a few minutes, I'm going to stop off at the office supply. I'm going to buy a couple of reams of fluorescent paper. Then I'm going to stay up late tonight designing and printing a nice flyer. Tomorrow morning, I'm going to start hanging those flyers on doors. You're all welcome to watch. I'll start right here, at six am. But I'm sure you'll all still have your lazy asses in bed. I won't." Then I turned to Deryl. "Have me some business cards printed ASAP, no title. Make them the same as these guys use." Then I turned back to the salesmen. "By the end of the week, I'll have a letter ready to send out to some of the nicer neighborhoods that I'm sure have good damage. I'll burn the midnight oil printing them and addressing the envelopes. Of course, you'll already be in bed long before I finish getting the first batch ready. Gentlemen, welcome to the big leagues. It's party time." And then I turned and left, without taking the time to gloat over their stunned expressions.

I didn't make one single sale the first week, so everyone enjoyed what they thought was going to be a great lesson for the boss. But three weeks into the month, I'd made 26 sales. I quit selling at that point, sure that they'd gotten the idea. They hadn't. Not a single one of them was still employed by my company two weeks after that month ended. They were non-believers. Sad, but Britt had not gotten them off to the right start. He hadn't shown them the pot of gold at the end of the rainbow and convinced each and every one of them that they could reach it. By the time I stepped in, it was too late for them. They were whipped puppies, just waiting to be beaten again.

You must sell the dream to your new salesmen. You have to show them the pot of gold at the end of the rainbow and make them believe that it is obtainable … and you have to do everything in your power to make sure that it is. We all need a dream.

Neal, Inc.—The Letter

Norfolk, Virginia, 1997. The first sales meeting at the office was conducted by Donny Haight, Marty's brother. He had already been in Virginia for a few weeks getting everything ready for us. The sales meeting was short and to the point.

"Everyone listen up. We've sent out a flyer and got almost no response. We've got telemarketers working, but they're getting very few leads. Evidently the local remodeling companies have been knocking on doors around here for years, and the homeowners are fed up with it. They don't like door-to-door salespeople. So, I don't know how the hell you're going to sell roofs here, but you'd better figure it out quick."

And the sales meeting was concluded. Damn, Donny always did know how to really pump up a group of salesmen and get them all giddy with excitement. But this time he'd outdone himself. I just sat there dumbfounded, wondering what I'd gotten myself into.

My wife was still teaching school, but she was out for the summer, so she was in Virginia with me. We met another salesman and his wife at a nearby diner the next morning for breakfast, and we were all still shaking our heads about the previous day's sales meeting.

As we were eating, an idea popped into my head, so I ran out to my truck and got a legal pad. When I got back inside, I ignored my food and the conversation at the table while I wrote a letter. I didn't like the way it sounded, so I tossed it and wrote another one. On the fifth or sixth try, I had something that I liked, so I let my wife read it. She thought it just might work.

After breakfast, we drove to Comp USA and spoke with one of the employees. He took us to the software section of the store, located and handed us a piece of software that was supposed to contain the names and addresses of millions and millions of people all over the country. He said we could search them by city and address. We bought the software and headed back to my little RV.

It took us all night to figure out how to use the software and how to merge the names and addresses into our word processor, but we finally got it figured out.

My idea was this: I wanted to send homeowners in a particular neighborhood a personal letter. The hard part would be getting them to actually read it, instead of simply chucking it as junk mail. To accomplish that, I wouldn't use mailing labels, I would print their name and address on their envelope. It would be a plain envelope without the company name or logo on it. The return address would have only my name, no address or company name. The letter inside would start: Dear Mr. _____, with their last name. Not Dear Homeowner or Dear Resident. Since each letter would be printed in black ink, I would sign each one in blue, so that the recipient could tell that I had personally signed it.

The content of the letter wasn't anything special—or at least I didn't think it was at the time. It simply explained: "Due to the hailstorm of a few weeks ago, many of your neighbors will be getting new roofs paid for by their insurance companies." No one wants to get left out. We all have to keep up with the Joneses, especially when it doesn't cost us anything.

The letter went on to explain that I was an "Insurance Claims Specialist," that I would inspect their roof and, if they had damage, I would work with their insurance company to get them a new roof. That was the gist of it anyway. I didn't want to hear from people who already had called their insurance company and filed a claim. I wanted to be part of it from the start. And I didn't want to hear: "No, I don't want you to handle it for me. I can do it myself." I wanted only those people who are intimidated enough by the thought of dealing with their insurance company to want an "expert" to handle it for them.

By the next evening, Deryl and I had printed off 300 letters and envelopes, signed, stuffed and stamped them. We used regular postage stamps, not bulk mail. And then we waited. I ran a phone cord through the window screen and mounted a telephone on the support beam of my large wooden porch swing. Then, for two days, I sat in the swing under the awning and chewed my fingernails.

On the afternoon of the third day, the phone started to ring. The problem was that the homeowners would pump me for information on the phone. So, I recorded a message on the answering machine and let it start taking the calls. Deryl would return them and set appointments for me.

She played dumb, telling them they would have to save their questions for me when I arrived for the appointment.

As a result of those first 300 letters, she set me 16 appointments. I sold 13 of them. One guy stood me up, and two of them didn't have any damage. Not bad, so I sent out another batch, and another. I would scout the neighborhoods that I wanted to target and write down the street names and the lowest and highest house numbers. I did that to avoid sending them to apartments or duplexes.

For the next three years, I sold almost exclusively off of the results of that letter. I would run leads from the office for the first two or three weeks of working a storm, to let some roofing activity begin in the neighborhoods, so that the recipients would know that the letter was for real. My closing ratio was usually 14 sales out of 15 appointments—very little wasted effort.

I have taught many other salesmen about the letter and how to use it. Most often they will report back to me that it didn't work for them. Then I'll find out that they used mailing labels, and letters that said Dear Homeowner, and envelopes with the company logo on them. They just didn't get it.

The point is that I took charge of my business. I became Neal, Inc. and refused to sit around and wait for the office to do everything for me. And I succeeded.

The Valpak Lady

Falls Church, Virginia, 2003. I was fairly new to NVR, having only been there two months or so. For lunch, I headed down to the nearest Subway. When I pulled into the parking lot, I noticed an SUV that had a Valpak magnetic sign on the door, and a lady sitting inside.

When I parked beside her and got out, I tapped on her window. She gave me a quick once over, then she saw the company name on my truck. She immediately smiled and rolled down her window. "Don't tell me that you're John Francis."

I was surprised that she knew him, or at least knew of him. I'd mentioned trying Valpak advertising to John and he'd blown off the idea quickly, saying, "Nah, it's not for us. The only people who go through those envelopes are the low-income coupon clippers. They can't afford us."

I told the lady no, that I wasn't John Francis, and then introduced myself. "You know John?"

Her expression turned into a frown. "No, I don't know him, but I've been trying to get in to see him for years. I can never get past the gatekeeper. And he won't return my calls."

I told her that I was interested in getting her in to meet with John and me, took her card and left.

After lunch, I sat in John's office. He still wasn't interested in talking about Valpak. Finally, I told him, "Look, she's a hottie, cute as hell. Do me a favor and let me schedule us a sit down with her, if for no other reason just so I can gawk at her bod while she's pitching us."

John laughed out loud for a long time and then finally agreed to let me set an appointment for her to come see us. In the several days leading up to the appointment, the office staff teased me unmercifully, especially Deryl.

But I had the last laugh. Not only did I get to do some gawking, but John liked her pitch and signed up for a few months with Valpak. It worked great, and it soon became one of the most cost effective forms of advertising in our portfolio. John cut back on much of his spending with other advertising sources so that he could sink more and more money into Valpak.

I don't think I ever told the Valpak lady how I'd finally convinced John to listen to her pitch, but knowing her, I'm sure she would have gotten a good laugh out of it.

Try to avoid practicing "contempt prior to investigation." Don't blow off things without at least taking a look at them.

Fighting The Good Fight

Appleton, Wisconsin, 1998. I had a customer who needed a new roof. It was a small house, with a small roof. He had enough hail damage for any reasonable insurance adjustor to pay for a complete new roof. The problem was, neither his adjustor nor his insurance company was reasonable.

I helped him file for re-inspection, but the insurance company sent the same adjustor out again, which totally defeats the purpose of a re-inspection. I had also instructed the company to make sure and call me so that I could meet the adjustor at the house. They didn't call me. They didn't call the customer either. In fact, they simply did as they had done the first time: they left him a note in his mailbox telling him that they found no damage and that they weren't going to approve his claim.

I called the adjustor and argued with him for a long time. When that didn't work, I called the insurance company. They were a local company, and I had already heard bad things about them. I talked to the manager in charge of claims several times, and I got nowhere. I talked to the vice president several times, and I got nowhere. Finally, I even managed to talk to the president of the company a couple of times, but I got nowhere with him either. They wouldn't even entertain the idea of sending out another adjustor to meet me at the customer's house.

I called and called and called. I bugged the hell out of them. Finally, the president of the company returned my call a final time, and after he told me again that the claim was closed and they weren't going to take any further action on it, I lost my temper. I was standing in a parking lot at the time and my wife was with me. I threatened to call the state insurance commission and file a complaint for "bad faith negotiation," but he wasn't impressed. Then, I saw the shock and horror on Deryl's face when she heard me tell the president of the insurance company, "Mr._____, before you hang up, I just want to be clear on something. I don't want there to be any misunderstanding on how I feel about you and your insurance company. If you were on fire, I wouldn't waste piss on you to put it out. Are we clear?"

Of course, after that, I knew that I wasn't going to get anywhere with them. So, I called David, a friend of mine at another roofing company, and asked him to meet me at the customer's house. After he'd inspected the roof and agreed that there was enough hail damage to justify the insurance company replacing it, I took him inside to meet the customer, explaining, "I've shot my wad with your insurance company. I've pissed them off so bad that I've become a detriment to your cause. I'm tearing up your contract with me, and I want you to sign up with David. Perhaps he'll have better luck with your insurance company than I did."

David didn't get anywhere with them either.

A month later, the customer called me and told me that he just got a check from his insurance company and he was ready for me to do his roof. When I asked how he had gotten them to pay, he told me that it had hailed again at his house and so he had filed a new claim. I was flabbergasted. I knew that it had hailed again, but it was tiny hail, pea size or smaller. It couldn't have damaged wet cardboard. Obviously, the president of the company had taken my threats more seriously than I'd thought and they were looking for a way out. The insurance company had used the excuse of the new hail to do the right thing—what they should have done in the first place.

But the story doesn't end there. A short time later, I got a call from a lady asking me to come out and meet her insurance adjustor and make sure he treated her fairly. I didn't know the lady, but I showed up. After meeting with her adjustor and negotiating the price for her, the adjustor wrote her a check and left.

"How did you get my name?" I asked her.

She laughed. "Neal, I'm sure you're familiar with _____ Insurance Company. Well, I work there in the claims department."

I winced. "And you called me? Christ, they must hate me over there."

"That's the understatement of the century. They've got a picture of you on the office dart board. No one is even allowed to mention your name out loud."

"But you don't have that insurance on your house," I said.

"Hell no, they're the worst f—ing insurance company there is. They fight every claim just as hard as they did with you."

"I still don't understand why you called me."

"Are you kidding? I've never seen anyone fight for a homeowner like you fought for that guy. You're like a bulldog. You just wouldn't give up. I made up my mind early on that you were the guy I wanted to help me with my insurance company. You're probably going to be getting a lot of calls from other people who work in that office. They all think you're great—that is, all except the ones who's asses you had your teeth sunk into."

All I could do was laugh.

When you know you're right, don't give up. Go the extra mile for your customers.

The Blind Man

Indianapolis, Indiana, 1996. A customer of mine took me to meet a friend of his that lived a few blocks down the street. The man was blind. I looked at his roof and determined that he had enough hail damage to justify his insurance company paying him for a new one. They did, and I turned the contract in to the office. The standing joke was: "Hell, getting him to sign up was easy, but getting him to pick the color of the shingles was a real bitch."

The man's house was a simple two-story box, straight up on all sides, with a large tree blocking the view of the tiny roof on the opposite side of the house from the driveway. You couldn't see that slope of the simple gable at all.

When we tore off the several layers of existing shingles, we discovered that the decking was planks instead of plywood, and they were all curled up, twisted, and some were rotted, especially on the driveway side of the house. The other side wasn't much better, but it wasn't quite as bad.

I went inside and explained the problem to the blind man. "If we don't re-deck it, it's going to look like crap. The curled up boards will hold the shingles up and it will look rough as hell." He didn't have the money to pay for something like that. Finally, I called his insurance adjustor, but before I did, I explained to the customer that the condition of the decking wasn't a result of the hailstorm, so the odds of getting the insurance company to foot the bill were slim at best.

The customer sat right there and listened to my end of the conversation with his adjustor. He heard me make a great case, then negotiate. I finally got the adjustor to pay for re-decking half the roof. After hanging up, I explained to the customer that we'd been very lucky to get as much as we did. Then I told him that I was going to re-deck the slope on the driveway side, which can be easily seen, and I won't do the opposite slope, because no one can see it anyway. It wasn't going to cost him anything out of his pocket. He was very happy.

When the job was finished, the driveway side looked perfect. The other side was rough, but you had to stand in one particular place and look up under and through the large tree to see it anyway, so it was no big deal. At least, it wasn't a big deal until I tried to collect.

A neighbor (who supposedly knew all about roofing) had come over and looked at the job. He told the customer that we'd done a terrible job on the back side of his roof. Of course, the neighbor hadn't seen it when it was torn off, so he didn't know what we'd had to work with. And the neighbor hadn't been privy to the conversation with the adjustor, and how I had done a masterful job of getting them to pay to re-deck half of the roof, when by rights they shouldn't have paid for any of it.

There was nothing I could say to make the customer believe that I had done right by him. He'd known his neighbor for many years, and he'd known me for a matter of weeks. He was convinced that I was a crook. Obviously, he had forgotten about the phone call I'd made to his adjustor and how happy he'd been that I got them to pay for a partial re-decking.

Finally, after a couple of weeks of fussing back and forth, the customer told me, "I called my insurance adjustor and asked him to come back out and look at the job. If he says I should pay you, I will."

A week later, the customer called me and told me, "Come get your f—ing money." When I showed up at his home, the customer's daughter wrote the check and handed it to her father. I could tell that it was prearranged. When he handed me the check, he held onto one end of it while he said, "You're a f—ing no good bastard, but my adjustor said pay you, so take your f—ing money and get the f—out of here and never come back."

I was devastated. I'd never had an unhappy customer—or at least I'd never quit on the job until they were happy. There was nothing I could say, nothing I could do, so I took the check and left.

Regardless of what you do, you can't please every customer. But that doesn't mean that you shouldn't try.

Bill Story's Story

Appleton, Wisconsin, 1998. I've told you the story of Joe Porto, the cantankerous, gruff old fart. He asked me to meet an adjustor at his sister's house and see that she was treated fairly. I did, and that's when I met Bill Story from Prudential Insurance.

I could tell right off that Bill wasn't a "catastrophe" adjustor who followed the hailstorms and hurricanes. He was a "staff" adjustor. He actually worked directly for Prudential instead of an independent adjustment firm. He was a very professional and distinguished looking man. We didn't like staff adjustors. They didn't know the game. They were on salary and didn't care if they ever approved a claim or if they ever made a contractor happy. Bill was dressed in nice slacks, shirt and tie ... and street shoes. Fortunately for him, the roof wasn't a steep one.

I put my ladder against the gutters and went on up, with Bill Story trailing right behind me. After looking around a bit and finding an awesome amount of hail damage, I glanced over at Bill, who seemed to be staring at one spot with a perplexed look on his face. Finally, he looked up at me and asked, "Neal, what does hail damage look like? I'm not sure I've ever seen any."

I spent the next fifteen minutes or so showing him how to distinguish hail damage from other imperfections on a shingle, and then he asked me, "Do you have time to show me how to measure a roof?"

Needless to say, we were up on that roof for almost two hours. At one point, Joe Porto yelled up at us, "You two taking a friggin nap or what?"

He didn't sound pleased, but then again, Joe Porto never sounded pleased about anything. I can just imagine him after sex, telling his partner in that same hateful growl, "Now turn your ass over and go to sleep." Of course, the image of Joe Porto having sex is not one that I relish the prospect of conjuring up, but that's another story.

Bill thanked me profusely for spending all of that time educating him. I gave him my card and told him not to hesitate to call me if he ran across something he didn't know how to handle. A week later, he called.

"Neal, I need a favor. I just finished inspecting a roof. It has a dark shingle, and I can't see the hail damage, if there is any. It's an important customer. He's a Prudential agent and he owns the highest volume agency in this part of the state. I don't want to give him something that he's not entitled to, but if he has damage I want to take care of him. If it's a borderline judgment call on the amount of damage, I'd like to give him the benefit of the doubt, but I have to take care of Prudential's money too. So I'd like you to make the determination for me. I've told him about you, and he said you can call him anytime. His name is Bruce."

After I agreed to help, Bill gave me Bruce's address and phone number. I don't know what Bill told Bruce about me, but I was welcomed with open arms. Later, I called Bill. "It really is a judgment call, but I can say with confidence that you wouldn't be cheating Prudential to buy Bruce a new roof." That made Bill very happy, and we installed Bruce a new roof. Bruce was very happy as well.

In the months that followed, I would get a call from Bruce. He'd give me the name of a customer who had called to file a claim. "Neal, before I file the paperwork, would you mind running by there and taking a look at it? Let me know if I should process the claim." I agreed, and reported back to him on my findings, which ran about 60–40 in favor of filing the claim. (Of course, the whole area had some degree of hail damage.)

Bruce's customers welcomed me with friendly smiles. "Bruce said you're the man who knows about this kind of thing. He trusts you, so we trust you. We'll accept whatever you say as gospel." If I found enough hail damage to tell Bruce to file the claim, Bill Story would go out to the customer's home, measure it, and approve the claim. He would then fax me the paperwork and tell me that I'd be getting a call from the customer. When they called, they already knew me, so it was usually a "Bring some samples out and let's get this thing rolling" kind of deal.

What better situation could a salesman be in? The homeowner's insurance agent sent me out with a good recommendation, and then their adjustor did the same. Those were lay down deals. Of course, I did a lot of pro-bono work too. I fixed small leaks without charging the customers, even if there wasn't enough hail damage to file a claim, and told the customers how lucky they were to have Prudential insurance. Bill and Bruce both appreciated that.

Later in the year, Bill Story was dispatched to Sheboygan, Wisconsin to work a big flood. He called me and asked, "Neal, I have to leave for a few weeks to work a flood down south of here, but we're still getting a few hail claims up here. I've already told the home office about you, and they agreed to let you handle the adjustments on the hail claims here for me, if you don't mind doing it. Will you help me out?"

Hell, talk about letting the fox loose in the hen house! Now I'd not only get to decide whether Prudential should pay for the roof, I'd get to set the price. Hell of a deal. I agreed, of course. While Bill was gone, I approved about 60 percent of the claims, and it may come as quite a shock to learn that I was the contractor on almost every one. Imagine that.

When Bill got back from working the flood, he told me how pleased the home office was with my work, and thanked me over and over.

I spent a short time in Minnesota the next year. My first call was to Bill Story. "Bill, do you guys have an office in Minneapolis and can you tell your adjustor here about me?" He was happy to oblige. Two years later, after another big hailstorm, I opened my own company in Oshkosh, Wisconsin. Bill Story threw a lot of business my way.

Please keep in mind that I never had as much as a cup of coffee with Bill Story or Bruce. They gave me business because I had earned their trust. They were both professionals, and I was a professional. We just got along on that basis.

Taking the time to help people is never wasted … and you never know how it will come back to you.

Hoyt's Temper

Appleton, Wisconsin, 1998. Hoyt, my good friend and housemate, called me and asked me to help him measure a condo building. It was a little over two stories to the gutter and he couldn't carry a long ladder on his truck. It was a very large roof for that area (300 squares), and he offered to split the deal with me for helping him.

After we'd spent hours and hours measuring the complicated roof and working up all of the necessary diagrams and paperwork, Hoyt set an appointment with the president of the condo association to get him to sign an agreement that would allow us to deal with their insurance company. Of course, the stipulation was, if the claim was approved and paid, we would get the job.

Hoyt and I drove over there separately. Deryl was with me, but she stayed in the truck while Hoyt and I met the customer in front of the large building. Hoyt did all of the talking. Before I knew what was happening, Hoyt was yelling at the customer, saying things like, "You're an idiot if you think we're going to do all of that work for you without a signed contract." And the customer was yelling back at him, "Well, you're an idiot if you think I'm going to sign a contract before the claim is approved."

The yelling didn't stop there. The two of them started really going at each other (verbally). It got really … heated. I shrugged and walked away. When I got back to my truck, I told Deryl, "Well, we can kiss this one goodbye." And I told her what was going on between Hoyt and the customer.

After the customer left, Hoyt came to my window. I teased him about needing to work on his "people skills" and his method of "cozying up to a customer." But he was still fuming and wasn't in any mood to joke about it.

A week later, Hoyt came home late and a bit tipsy. Deryl and I were watching TV. He stood between us and the TV, pulled a contract out from behind his back, and slammed it down on the coffee table. "Never question my sales ability again," he said confidently. "I know how to handle an idiot customer." It was a signed contract on the condo roof.

Having Fun With Hoyt

Appleton, Wisconsin, 1998. Hoyt called me to bring over a long ladder so he could get up on a little two-story house. The house had a 4–12 front slope, but the front yard fell away toward the street, and there was a large tree hindering access to that slope. The back slope was 7–12, but the ground on that side was level, so I put the ladder up in the back.

Hoyt went up the ladder, scampered to the ridge, did his measurements, and started back down. Hoyt was never comfortable walking on roofs with any pitch to them. This one wasn't too steep, but the shingles were very old. Every time he took a step toward the ladder, his shoes slipped on the loose granules, so he jumped back to the ridge. After watching him make several attempts, I went up the ladder.

Hoyt isn't a big guy, so I grabbed the eave and pulled myself, and the top of the ladder, firmly to the gutter, effectively securing it so that it wouldn't move if he slid down and into it. Then I urged him, "This ladder isn't going anywhere. Just come on down. If you slide, I'll catch you." But he just couldn't force himself to do it. (It would be another year before we discovered the magic of Cougar Paws.)

Then an idea hit me. I could have a little fun. I told Hoyt to sit tight and I'd get him a rope. I had one in my truck, a long one with knots in it to hang onto. I used it for safety on steep roofs. I went down the ladder and stood under the eave where Hoyt couldn't see me. Then I called Bobby Powers and every salesman I could get on the phone, telling them the address and that Hoyt was stranded on a roof.

Within minutes, trucks started pulling up from every direction. Bobby scolded me, "Neal, just move the ladder around to the front."

"Are you kidding? I can't pass up an opportunity like this. It's just too good."

Bobby laughed and tied one end of the rope to the tree. I tossed the other end, which had a baseball hooked to it, up to Hoyt. He used the rope to get back down to the ladder, to the welcoming jeers, cheers, and clapping of the audience I'd assembled.

Hoyt never did forgive me for that one.

A Personal Story

How many estimates does the average roofing salesman give in his first three weeks out of training—20, 30, surely not 40?

Bobby Powers had told me my first day on the job in Indianapolis, "Neal, if you give ten estimates every day, you'll make more money than you ever dreamed of making." But my brain works differently. I was thinking, "I'm not as good as the other salesmen. If most guys have to give ten estimates to succeed, I'd better give 15."

So that's what I did. I would start early, pick a neighborhood and park my truck in a central location. Then I would carry my ladder down the sidewalk, leaving it out near the street when I went up to the door. "I'm in the neighborhood doing free roof inspections for hail damage from the big storm that hit a while back. Would you like me to look at yours and give you a free estimate if you have damage?"

I tried to keep at it until I had given 15 estimates, but some days it just couldn't be done. If I fell short, I would do my best to make it up the next day, or on Saturday. I cut the number to eight on Sunday, because I didn't start until after noon. Sometimes I was still knocking on doors well after dark, lining up estimates for the next day so that I'd get off to a good start. I gave many, many estimates in the rain.

Do the math: fifteen a day, six days a week, and eight on Sunday. That's 98 estimates a week. I did that for three weeks. That's 294 estimates (probably more like 250 because I didn't always reach my goal).

As a footnote, you may find it amusing to learn that, out of those first 250 estimates, I sold ZERO! Like I said, I had no talent for sales. Bobby Powers had shown me how to measure a roof and write up an estimate, but not how to actually "sell" a roof. When I finally caught him in the office and told him that I feared that I was doing something wrong, he asked me to tell him exactly what I was doing.

"Well, I look at the roof and if there is damage, I measure it and then go back to my truck and write up the estimate. Then I give it to the home-owner."

"What do you say when you hand it to him?" Bobby asked me.

"I say, 'Here's your estimate. If you have any questions, give me a call.'"

Bobby rolled his eyes and shook is head. "Go get in my truck. I guess I forgot to show you how to sell a damn roof."

After seeing how the sales process actually worked, I went back out with a renewed excitement. I sold 99 roofs in the next four months. I also set my personal record of selling six in one day. It took me another two years to break that record.

In early December of that year, Bobby Powers called me at my apart-ment in Red Oak, Texas. "Marty and I are going shopping for our wives' Christmas presents. We want you to come with us."

I agreed, so they picked me up in front of my apartment. I rode in the back. On the way to the mall, Bobby and Marty were talking about good salesmen they'd had over the years. After some discussion, Marty asked, "Who do think is the best we've ever had?"

Bobby answered, "Tom Boyle. He was a real racehorse. That guy could sell anything to anyone for any price."

Marty laughed. "No, the best we've ever had is the guy sitting in the back seat."

Bobby choked and coughed and then said, "Neal? He couldn't sell his way out of a wet paper bag." (We were friends, so he knew he wouldn't hurt my feelings … too much.)

Marty replied, "He can't sell as many as some of the others, but he can actually collect on the ones he sells. That's what makes him the best. We never have to worry about collecting his jobs."

Nothing anyone has ever said about me before or since has made me more proud than that. And it meant more because it was Marty who said it. I liked him, and respected him … and I still do. At the time of this writing, Deryl and I are within days of moving back to Texas to help Marty build, equip, staff, and organize his new corporate office.

Making sales is the easy part. Making happy customers is the real challenge.

◆   ◆   ◆

So those are my stories, or at least a few of them. (Obviously, I have a lot more.) I hope you enjoyed them, and I hope that you garnered some useful tips from hearing about my experiences. You probably have your own stories. In fact, if you've been in the roofing business very long, I'm sure that you do. Use them to help teach your people important lessons, to get them thinking, to caution them, to inspire them … or just to give them a good laugh.

The End

About the Author

In the mid 1980s, due to circumstances of my own making, I was dead broke, living in my car, and hustling pool in the bars every night for food and gas money. Of course I purchased those only if there was enough money left over after my craving for alcohol was momentarily satisfied.

By December of 1993, I was sick and tired of being sick and tired, so I stumbled through the door of an AA meeting. By early 1996, I had begun to get my life back together. I was a security guard, making $6.50 per hour and working 75 to 90 hours a week to pay the bills. But I was sober and feeling good about myself again. My life took another dramatic turn in March of that year.

◆　　◆　　◆

I was recruited into the roofing business as a salesman by Bobby Powers in 1996 in Red Oak, Texas. I was 43, late in life by most standards, especially since I knew absolutely nothing about roofing or construction. I was given 45 minutes of training in the field, which consisted of how to measure a very simple roof and write up an estimate. That was fairly typical training for salesmen in a "storm chasing" roofing company. Two weeks later, we were off to Indianapolis, Indiana to work a big hailstorm.

I asked a lot of questions, and at one point I was told by one of the managers, "Neal, if you'd spend more time out there knocking on doors and less time in here asking stupid questions, you'd sell a lot more roofs." I have no idea how I survived. I do know, however, that I feel very guilty for allowing those customers to believe that I knew what I was talking about. When one would ask me about Ice and Water Shield, since I wasn't sure what it was or what it was used for, I would simply tell them, "If the roof is installed properly, you don't really need it." Unfortunately for them, they believed me.

For the next four years I averaged selling over a hundred roofs per season, with my season lasting anywhere from five to eight months. My personal record was seven in one day. I still only knew about roofing what I'd picked up from watching the crews do the jobs I sold. The money was decent though, and I could pretty much set my own schedule. I could decide when to quit for the year and head home. I spent the winters in Texas, playing golf and traveling to places my wife, Deryl, and I had never been able to afford before. By the beginning of the third year, Deryl was able to quit her teaching job and come on the road with me. She still works with me today.

After my fourth year of selling, Marty, the owner of the company, encouraged me to go into business for myself. He became my silent partner and made his line of credit with the suppliers available to me. The first year went okay. We made some money, and I learned a lot. The experience also made me feel more confident about being out on my own, so by mutual agreement, Marty and I dissolved our partnership. The following year, I opened offices in Illinois, and Nebraska, to go with the one I already had in Wisconsin. One year of that was enough to shoot my stress level off the scale, and Mother Nature gave me a wake up call. I ended up in a hospital emergency room with nurses sticking nitro tablets under my tongue and a very nice little drip, drip, drip of morphine going into my arm. It turned out not to be a serious thing—"a stress-related event." Call it what you will, I thought I'd bought the farm. The money wasn't enough to justify going through all of that, so I decided to go back to work for someone else. I have never regretted that decision.

A few weeks later, I went to work for an Indianapolis based company. I reorganized their corporate office and then opened them up four new offices in three states. That was a crazy year. After I'd finished doing what they'd hired me to do, I once again bumped into Bobby Powers, this time in Columbus, Ohio. When he heard that I was about to be unemployed, he told me about John Francis, the owner of Northern Virginia Roofing.

"Neal, he needs you. He's a great guy with a nice business, but his office is as unorganized as any I've ever seen. Promise me you won't take another job until you meet John."

Bobby was right. John was a nice guy ... and an honest one. And he was right about the state of John's office. It was a mess. John and I came to an agreement, and Deryl and I both joined NVR in May of 2003. I have since done both short term and long term consulting work with roofing companies from southern Virginia to the Pocono Mountains of Pennsylvania.

As strange as it may sound, the contents of this book are based almost exclusively on what I have learned since 2002. The "storm chasing" side of the business and the "permanent local company" side of the business are barely similar. I am writing this book for the latter.

The principles contained herein are valid, tested, and proven in a variety of companies, in a variety of circumstances, from the fast-paced and highly competitive marketplace of the Washington, D.C. Metro area, to small markets like Stroudsburg, PA, population five thousand. It's not a theory, or a speculation, or a hypothesis. It simply works.

Mike Larkin, the Elk shingle manufacturer's rep, summed it up during our trip to tour Elk's newest factory in Moorestown, PA. He said, "Neal, you know that I play in a soccer league with a bunch of guys from the top roofing companies in the D.C. area. Every time NVR is mentioned, they spit and gag and curse. They say, 'We're already giving estimates that are hundreds of dollars less than NVR's, but they still keep getting the jobs. We don't know how to compete with them.'" What could I do but laugh?

One last point: Since 1996 not a year has gone by in which I haven't sold roofs. My first four years in the business were spent selling roofs. When I owned my own company, I sold roofs. When I set up offices for other companies, I sold roofs. When I managed or consulted for companies, I sold roofs. I have sold roofs in:

Indianapolis, Indiana; Virginia Beach, Virginia; Appleton, Wisconsin; Centreville, Virginia; Denver, Colorado; Dallas/Fort Worth Metroplex, Texas; Oshkosh, Wisconsin; Chicago, Illinois; Cincinnati, Ohio; Louisville, Kentucky; Lafayette, Louisiana; Omaha, Nebraska; Stroudsburg, Pennsylvania; and the Washington, D.C. Metropolitan area.

Sales are the heartbeat of our business. I can't train a salesman in a new market if I haven't sold roofs there. I have heard the words, "Oh yeah, that technique may work where you're from, but it won't work here." I heard those exact words from the salesmen at NVR when I got there. So, I went out and sold a bunch of roofs. Then I called a sales meeting and told them, "Okay, now I've sold roofs here, and it's no different than anywhere else. So, we're going to do it my way." A few months later, they had all quit or been fired. I hired new ones and trained them my way. Many of those are still with NVR today and doing very well.

The formula in this book is not market specific. It will work virtually anywhere.

978-0-595-43387-2
0-595-43387-1